The Leaders You Leave Behind

Mission First, People Always

A Practical Framework for Leadership That Endures

ROBERT MOORE

Printed in the United States of America

Edited by Peter Letzelter
Designed and typeset by Caerus Kourt

ISBN 979-8-9947503-0-8 [Hardback]
ISBN 979-8-9947503-1-5 [Paperback]
ISBN 979-8-9947503-2-2 [EBook]

First Edition

Table of Contents

Foreword v

Introduction: *Two Worlds, One Truth* 1

Chapter 1: *Mission First, People Always* 11

Chapter 2: *Lead by Example: Actions Over Words* 35

Chapter 3: *Empower and Trust: Decentralized Leadership* 57

Chapter 4: *Discipline and Standards: The Framework of Excellence* 79

Chapter 5: *Communication: The Leader's Essential Tool* 101

Chapter 6: *Adaptability: Leading Through Change* 139

Chapter 7: *Develop Future Leaders: The Legacy of Leadership* 173

Chapter 8: *Bringing It All Together: Your Leadership Philosophy* 197

Afterword: *The Future* 211

About the Author 213

Foreword

I write books for two reasons.

The first is to share what I have learned. Over the course of my career—as a soldier, a noncommissioned officer, a commissioned officer, a technology leader, and a nonprofit leader—I have been fortunate to learn from extraordinary leaders and from difficult experiences. Leadership lessons accumulate slowly over time. Some come from success. Many more come from failure, reflection, and the willingness to try again. Writing is one way I attempt to capture those lessons and pass them along to others who are walking their own leadership journeys.

But there is a second reason I write that is just as important.

I write to remind myself of the kind of leader I should be.

Leadership is not a destination where someone arrives and remains permanently competent, wise, and effective. Leadership is a daily practice. Every leader—no matter how experienced—has moments where they fall short of their own standards. I certainly have. I have made decisions too quickly, communicated poorly, failed to listen when I should have, and missed opportunities to support people who needed it.

Writing about leadership forces me to slow down and reflect on the principles that should guide my actions. In that sense, this book is as much a reminder to myself as it is guidance for anyone else. I am not presenting a picture of perfect leadership. I am describing the leadership I strive toward, knowing full well that I will continue to fall short at times.

Many of the ideas in this book are rooted in military leadership principles. I grew up professionally in an Army culture that emphasized responsibility, discipline, development, and care for the people entrusted to you. Those principles shaped my understanding of leadership long before I ever held a civilian leadership role.

Some readers may notice that the military leadership philosophy described in these pages may not always resemble what we see in today's political or senior military leadership environments. That observation is fair. Institutions evolve. Leaders change. The world itself changes constantly.

But the leadership principles described here are not about personalities or politics. They are about timeless ideas that have proven effective in organizations for generations. Concepts like leading by example, developing future leaders, maintaining discipline and standards, communicating clearly, and caring for the people who carry the mission forward.

The reality is that not every leader embraces these ideas. Some leaders prioritize authority over trust. Others pursue results while neglecting the people responsible for achieving them. Still others attempt to please everyone and lose sight of the mission entirely.

The difference between these approaches is often visible. Teams led by leaders who truly believe in *mission first, people always* tend to become stronger over time. They develop capability. They build trust. They produce results while developing the people who make those results possible. Teams led without those principles may still achieve short-term success, but they often struggle to sustain it.

This book is my attempt to describe the leadership approach that I have seen work repeatedly across very different environments—from military units to school districts, from technology departments to nonprofit organizations.

If you read this book looking for a formula that guarantees perfect leadership, you will not find one.

If you read it looking for principles that can help you become a better leader tomorrow than you were yesterday, then I hope you will find something valuable here.

Leadership is difficult work. It demands humility, courage, discipline, and care for others. None of us will ever practice it perfectly. But every day gives us another opportunity to try. And that is enough to keep learning, keep leading, and keep moving forward.

Introduction

Two Worlds, One Truth

As a Staff Sergeant in Iraq in 2006, I learned that combat leadership required both decisive action and deep empathy. Soldiers needed a leader to make tough decisions under pressure, which was a principle drilled into me since my early days as an Army Private and intelligence analyst in Korea. Yet, they also needed someone who truly cared about them, and not just as tactical assets. Servant leadership was an idea I was just beginning to understand.

The best leaders aren't those who just bark orders. They earn loyalty by combining tactical and technical excellence with genuine care for people. This tension between authority and service defined my career, shaping both my military and post-military leadership, and is the basis of this book's philosophy.

The Journey That Shaped This Book

My path through military leadership was anything but straightforward. As an intelligence analyst, I learned that leadership stems from insight about the terrain, the adversary, and, crucially, the people beside you. In Korea, and later with the 82nd Airborne, I saw that the best leaders continually learn and listen.

As a non-commissioned officer (NCO) operating in the psychological operations (PSYOP) space, I gained a clearer understanding of leadership's human side. PSYOP isn't about forcing compliance; it's about understanding motivation, culture, and how to influence, not decree. My 2006 deployment to Iraq proved that the most effective leaders earn trust and serve missions larger than themselves, rather than relying on rank.

A key point in my career was earning a direct commission. Moving from enlisted to officer gave me a new perspective. I had led from the middle as an NCO; now, I would lead from a different level in the organization structure.

When I left the military as a Captain, I had led in tactical and training commands, as well as special operations and conventional teams, both as an NCO and an officer. Each role taught me something new about leadership and revealed more of the puzzle.

THE UNEXPECTED CLASSROOM

When I left the military and entered the civilian technology sector, I assumed my leadership education was complete. I was wrong. As a software company manager, I led teams in tech support, user technology, data conversion, and technical writing. This work demanded technical skill and revealed the pressures of the private sector. Then, as the tech bubble burst in the early 2000s, I was laid off. That was something the military hadn't prepared me for.

The pink slip hit harder than I expected. My confidence, built through years of military service and early civilian success, took a beating. For the first time in my professional life, I questioned whether I had what it took.

But sometimes the best leadership lessons come from our lowest moments.

As a network technician in a public school district, I found my calling. For thirteen years, I supported teachers and students while immersing myself in the world of education technology.

One day, I walked into my boss's office. He was the CIO of one of the largest public school districts in the state, and I asked him a direct question: "What do I need to do to get your job someday?"

His answer surprised me. "Leave."

He explained that I needed to get a CIO job in a smaller district first to gain the executive experience I would need to lead a larger one. It was hard advice, but exactly what I needed.

While searching for that opportunity, I started my MBA. Just before finishing graduate school, I was hired as CIO for a smaller district. For two and a half years, I led technology operations, working with diverse stakeholders to support the educational mission. Every challenge, success, and failure taught me more about leadership.

When my former boss retired, I applied for the position I'd discussed with him years earlier. I got the job. My new role gave me responsibility for over seventy people and a budget exceeding $10 million. For the first time in my civilian career, I managed other managers, building a team of leaders to carry out our mission. The responsibility felt both familiar and entirely new.

During my tenure, team members and the department as a whole earned awards for excellence at both the state and national levels. But the achievement I'm most proud of wasn't recognition. It was watching my team members grow, develop, and become leaders themselves.

THE BRIDGE BETWEEN TWO WORLDS

Looking back, from my intelligence unit in Korea to a PSYOP unit in Iraq, from my first civilian management job to leading a large technology department, I see one fundamental truth about leadership: The principles that made leaders effective in military operations are the same that make servant leaders in other organizations effective today.

This claim may seem odd. Military and servant leadership could be seen as opposites. Military leadership is typecast as top-down, mission-focused, and uncompromising. Servant leadership is characterized as compassionate, bottom-up, and focused on people.

But that's a false dichotomy.

The best military leaders I served under in the 1990s and 2000s, from the Cold War to the Global War on Terror, knew that *you accomplish the mission through people, not despite them.* They were demanding, yet compassionate. They upheld high standards. They supported development. They made hard decisions. Above all, they cared about those affected by those decisions. In the civilian world, I learned that genuine care must lead to real results. Servant leadership without mission accomplishment isn't leadership, it's just being nice. The synthesis of these two philosophies, military effectiveness and servant-hearted compassion, is what this book explores.

The Whys of My Book

WHY MILITARY LEADERSHIP?

You might wonder why I focus specifically on military leadership philosophy, specifically from the 1990s, rather than contemporary doctrine. The answer is both personal and practical. The 1990s were unique for military leaders. After Vietnam, the Army was rebuilt around professional standards, operational excellence, and values-based leadership. Leaders like General Colin Powell shaped principles to balance mission and care for soldiers. The Army stressed development, ethical decision-making, and the idea that leaders eat last, figuratively and literally.

This was the leadership culture I entered as a young soldier. These were the principles modeled by the NCOs and officers who shaped my understanding of what good leadership looks like. And importantly, these principles were tested in real-world operations, from Desert Storm to the Balkans, and proved their effectiveness in both combat and peacetime environments. Leadership doctrine in the 1990s was less bureaucratic than it is today. It focused on timeless principles over process, trusted leaders' judgment, and saw leadership as an art as much as a science.

These principles translate remarkably well to civilian contexts, precisely because they're rooted in human nature rather than military-specific action.

WHY SERVANT LEADERSHIP?

Servant leadership, as articulated by Robert Greenleaf and developed by practitioners like Ken Blanchard and Simon Sinek, offers a powerful counterbalance to command-and-control models. At its core, servant leadership inverts the traditional hierarchy; leaders exist to serve their teams, not the other way around.

This philosophy has resonated with me throughout my career. I've learned that sustainable influence stems from understanding and serving your audience's needs. It became more powerful when I realized that my primary job wasn't to be served by my soldiers or employees; rather, my responsibility was to create the conditions for their success.

Servant leadership addresses the limitations of pure military or directive leadership models because:

- It prioritizes people development.
- It emphasizes listening before directing.
- It builds commitment through trust rather than compliance through authority.
- It recognizes that the leader's role is to remove obstacles, not create them.

But servant leadership also has vulnerabilities. Without the structure, accountability, and decisiveness of military leadership, servant leaders can become permissive, avoid difficult decisions, and fail to maintain standards.

The synthesis of these two philosophies creates something more powerful than either alone.

WHY NOW

We're experiencing a leadership crisis in America and around the world. Research as recent as 2025 showed that workers don't want to move to management. Organizations are struggling to find leaders who can both achieve results and earn genuine loyalty. Employee engagement is at historic lows. Turnover is costly and constant. Many people don't trust their leaders, and many leaders feel isolated and ineffective.

At the same time, we're seeing a hunger for a different kind of leadership. People want leaders who are strong but not harsh, decisive but not dismissive, and ambitious but not self-serving. They want leaders who get things done while making the workplace better, not worse.

This book offers a path forward. I've developed a framework that works in any context, military or civilian, corporate or nonprofit, large organization or small team.

I know it works because I've lived it. I've applied these principles in combat zones and school board meetings, used them in leading special operations soldiers and managing IT professionals, and practiced them in environments where failure meant lives lost and environments where failure meant disappointed stakeholders.

The principles remain the same; the results are consistent.

What You'll Find in This Book

I've intentionally designed this book to be an introduction and a foundation for leaders. Each chapter presents the core principle of an effective leadership philosophy, explained clearly and applied practically:

- **Chapter 1. Mission First, People Always**: Tackles the false choice between results and relationships. You'll learn how to hold both in tension and why that tension is productive, not problematic. I examine the military's *mission first, people always* philosophy, and show how taking care of people *is* mission accomplishment.
- **Chapter 2. Lead by Example: Actions Over Words**: Shows how to model excellence while building credibility through consistent behavior. You'll discover why actions speak louder than any speech or written policy, and how to align what you do with what you say.
- **Chapter 3. Empower and Trust: Decentralized Leadership**: Explores how to distribute authority throughout an organization and develop decision-makers at every level. This chapter challenges the modern assumption

that leaders must control everything, showing instead how to create conditions where others can lead.

- **Chapter 4. Discipline and Standards: The Framework of Excellence**: Challenges modern assumptions that structure and freedom are opposites. You'll discover how clear standards will actually empower teams and why discipline sets people free to excel.
- **Chapter 5. Communication: The Leader's Essential Tool**: Examines how to ensure clarity, build trust, and navigate the complex landscape of modern organizational communication. You'll learn when to use different communication methods and why listening is the most powerful tool in the leadership arsenal.
- **Chapter 6. Adaptability: Leading Through Change**: Equips you to navigate uncertainty while staying grounded in core principles. This chapter shows how to lead through crisis, strategic shifts, and cultural transformations without losing organizational identity.
- **Chapter 7. Develop Future Leaders: The Legacy of Leadership**: Shifts the focus from short-term task completion to long-term organizational capacity. You'll learn to measure success by who your people become, not just what they do, and discover how to create a culture where leadership development is everyone's responsibility.
- **Chapter 8. Bringing It Together: Your Leadership Philosophy**: Synthesizes the seven principles into a coherent framework and guides the creation of a Personal Leadership Constitution. This chapter helps you move from understanding principles to living them consistently.

Each chapter is practical and actionable. You won't find academic theory disconnected from reality. Instead, there are principles forged in the crucible of real leadership scenarios, from military operations to managing technology transformation in public education.

HOW TO USE THIS BOOK

It is written for leaders at every level, from the newly promoted supervisor wondering how to earn respect to the seasoned executive looking to refine their approach. Whether you're in the military, corporate world, nonprofit sector, education, or anywhere else people need to be led, these principles apply.

I encourage you to read it through once to grasp the complete framework, then return to individual chapters when facing specific leadership challenges. Take notes. Argue with me in the margins. Test these principles against your own experience.

Most importantly, apply what you learn. Leadership is not a theoretical discipline; it's a practice, developed through daily decisions and tested in the fire of real responsibility.

The Journey Ahead

Leadership is hard. If it were easy, everyone would do it well, and we wouldn't have the leadership crisis we're facing today. But leadership is also learnable. I'm living proof. I wasn't born with natural charisma or exceptional talent. I made plenty of mistakes along the way. Some were in training environments where the cost was low, others in real-world situations where the stakes were higher.

What I learned—through military service and civilian leadership, through success and failure, through leading in combat and leading in conference rooms, through classrooms and on the job—is that effective leadership comes down to a consistent set of principles, faithfully applied. Whether leading a team in a combat zone, a department in a corporation, a nonprofit serving the community, or a school district technology department, the fundamentals remain the same: character, mission focus, service, discipline, trust, development, courage, and legacy.

Master these, and you'll become the kind of leader people choose to follow, not just the person they're required to obey.

Chapter 1

Mission First, People Always

Mission first, people always. It was probably in the Army that I first heard that phrase. If you think "mission first" means sacrificing soldiers unnecessarily or pushing your people too hard, you don't understand leadership. *Mission first, people always.* They aren't competing priorities; they're inseparable.

I didn't fully understand what it meant the first time I heard it. It would take years of experience, and mistakes, before I grasped the profound truth in those words.

The Paradox That Isn't a Paradox

On the surface, *mission first, people always* sounds contradictory. How can the mission come first if people always matter? Doesn't putting the mission first mean sometimes sacrificing people's needs?

This apparent contradiction reveals a fundamental misunderstanding about leadership. The phrase isn't describing a conflict between two competing values. It's describing two dimensions of the same responsibility:

- **Mission first**: Means that accomplishing the organization's objectives is nonnegotiable. Whether leading a military unit, a technology department, or a customer service team, you have a job to do. Resources are invested in the team because there's work that needs to be accomplished. Deadlines matter. Quality matters. Results matter.
- **People always**: Means that accomplishing the mission must always account for the human beings doing the work. It means recognizing that people aren't just resources to be consumed, they're the reason the mission can be accomplished at all.

The breakthrough insight is that *taking care of your people is mission accomplishment.*

The military often has a relentless operational tempo. Missions come daily, often with minimal notice. The pressure is constant. Some leaders respond by pushing their teams harder and harder, cutting corners on rest, ignoring signs of stress, and treating people as expendable assets.

Those units suffer. They have higher injury rates, more disciplinary problems, lower morale, and, critically, they make more mistakes. When people are exhausted, stressed, and feel uncared for, they don't perform at their best. The mission suffers.

Other leaders—the ones I came to respect most—understood that maintaining their people's readiness was essential to mission success. They fought for adequate rest cycles. They paid attention to individual struggles. They ensured their soldiers had what they needed. And their units performed better, consistently.

The lesson was clear. Caring for people isn't a nice extra when you have the time. It's a mission requirement.

THE MILITARY'S MISSION-FIRST HERITAGE

The US military has always been a mission-focused organization. It exists to accomplish specific national security objectives. Every training exercise, equipment purchase, and organizational structure is designed with mission accomplishment in mind.

The 1990s military, the force that emerged victorious from the Cold War and demonstrated overwhelming capability in Desert Storm, exemplified this mission focus. It was a professional, competent force that took its responsibilities seriously.

But the best leaders of that era understood something crucial: mission *focus* doesn't mean mission *obsession* at the expense of everything else. They recognized that sustainable mission accomplishment requires healthy, capable, motivated people.

I saw this firsthand during my time with the 82nd Airborne. The entire culture was built around readiness, being prepared to deploy anywhere in the world within hours. That kind of readiness demands discipline, training, and sacrifice.

Yet the Division's best leaders weren't the ones who simply drove their soldiers the hardest. They were the ones who understood that true readiness comes from well-trained, properly equipped, adequately rested, and genuinely committed soldiers.

A tired paratrooper who hates his leadership is a liability, not an asset. The leaders need paratroopers who are sharp, capable, and committed. That means taking care of them.

As a mature leader later in my military career, I fought for training resources. I ensured we had time to maintain equipment properly. I tried to get to know my soldiers. When someone had a personal crisis, I helped them handle it. And when it was time to jump out of airplanes or execute a mission, people trusted me.

That's *mission first, people always* in action.

THE SERVANT LEADERSHIP CONNECTION

Servant leadership, a philosophy articulated by Robert Greenleaf in the 1970s, begins with a fundamentally different question than traditional leadership models. Instead of asking, "How do I get people to accomplish my objectives?" a servant leader asks, "How do I help people grow and succeed while accomplishing our shared objectives?"

At first glance, this might seem incompatible with military leadership's mission focus. Servant leadership sounds soft, focused on feelings and personal development. Military leadership sounds hard, focused on objectives and results.

Again, this is a false dichotomy.

The truth is that servant leadership enhances mission accomplishment. When leaders genuinely serve their people—by removing obstacles, providing resources, developing capabilities, and caring about individual growth—those people become more capable, more committed, and more effective.

Consider what servant leadership actually involves:

- **Listening actively**: To understand what people need and what challenges they face. This isn't touchy-feely nonsense; it's intelligence gathering. How can you lead effectively without knowing what's really happening in the organization?
- **Empowering others**: To make decisions and take initiative. This isn't abdication of responsibility; it's force multiplication. The more capable decision-makers are developed, the more the organization can accomplish.
- **Building community**: Where people support each other. This isn't just team-building for its own sake; it's creating resilience and redundancy for critical systems and tasks.

Strong teams can handle challenges that would break a collection of individuals.

- **Developing people's capabilities**: Through training, mentoring, and challenging assignments. This isn't a distraction from the mission; it's building the capacity to handle future missions.

Every aspect of servant leadership directly contributes to mission accomplishment. The servant leader recognizes that the route to exceptional organizational performance runs through the growth and development of the people they are responsible for.

Taking Care of People ***Is*** *Mission Accomplishment*

Let me be explicit about why people-focused leadership isn't separate from mission accomplishment, but rather central to it.

PEOPLE ARE YOUR CAPABILITY

An organization's capability to accomplish anything is entirely dependent on its people. You don't have a technology department's worth of capacity; you have the combined skills, knowledge, and effort of team members. You don't have a unit's combat power; you have what trained soldiers can execute.

Every investment in people's skills, health, readiness, and motivation is an investment in organizational capacity. Every time people are damaged through neglect, overwork, or poor leadership, the organization's capacity to perform is diminished.

When I was the network technician working toward becoming a CIO, my supervisor understood this principle. He invested in developing my skills beyond what the immediate job required. He allowed me to take on challenging projects. Was this a distraction from our department's immediate mission? No, it was building the capability of our department for the future. He was developing me, and in doing so, strengthening the entire organization.

DISCRETIONARY EFFORT MATTERS

There's a massive difference between people who do the minimum required and people who give their best effort. In any organization, the majority of real value comes from people's discretionary effort, the extra initiative, creativity, and commitment they choose to give.

You cannot command discretionary effort. You can't order someone to care. You can't mandate innovation or initiative.

But you can earn it. When people feel genuinely cared for, when they trust their leaders, when they see that their growth and well-being matter, they choose to give more. They stay late to solve a problem. They suggest improvements. They mentor newer team members. They go the extra mile because they want to, not because they have to.

During my time as CIO, I saw this pattern repeatedly. Team members who felt valued and supported consistently outperformed those who felt like interchangeable parts. The difference wasn't in their job descriptions or their assigned tasks. It was in their level of engagement and commitment.

RETENTION EQUALS CAPABILITY PRESERVATION

Losing a trained, experienced person is expensive. All the time invested in training them, all the knowledge they've accumulated, all the relationships they've built—it all walks out the door with them.

In the military, we understood this viscerally. Training a skilled intelligence analyst or a competent NCO takes years. Losing them to poor leadership means starting over with someone new. It means reduced capability during the training period. It means institutional knowledge lost.

The same is true in civilian organizations. When good people leave because they feel undervalued or poorly led, an organization becomes less capable. When they stay because they feel cared for and see a future, an organization becomes stronger over time.

Taking care of people, helping them grow, valuing their contributions, supporting them through challenges—this isn't just nice. It's how to maintain and build organizational capability.

MISSION DEMANDS SUSTAINABLE PERFORMANCE

Some missions are sprints: intense, short-duration efforts that demand everything you have. But most organizational work is a marathon. A team needs to perform well month after month, year after year.

High performance cannot be sustained when constantly burning people out. Readiness is not maintained by treating people as disposable. Long-term missions with a team that's exhausted, demoralized, and counting the days until they can leave will not lead to mission accomplishment.

Sustainable performance requires balancing periods of intense effort with adequate recovery. It requires maintaining people's health—physical, mental, and emotional. It requires helping people find meaning and satisfaction in the work, not just enduring it until they can escape.

This isn't soft leadership. It's realistic leadership that accounts for human limitations and needs.

The Balance in Practice

Understanding that mission and people aren't competing priorities is one thing. Actually leading with both in mind is another. How do you make this work in practice?

START WITH MISSION CLARITY

Everything begins with absolute clarity about what you're trying to accomplish. A team needs to understand:

- What is the mission?
- Why does it matter?
- What does success look like?
- What are the priorities?

Without mission clarity, you can't make good decisions about anything else. Every choice about resource allocation—whose development to prioritize, which projects to tackle— depends on understanding what you're trying to accomplish.

When I took over as CIO for the first time, I spent time ensuring that everyone on the team understood our core mission, which was supporting teaching and learning through reliable, effective technology. Every other consideration—projects, priorities, budget decisions—had to serve that mission.

This clarity didn't constrain us; it liberated us. When someone proposed a project, we could evaluate it against our mission. When we had to make tough resource decisions, we had criteria for choosing. Mission clarity made better decisions possible.

INVEST IN PEOPLE'S CAPABILITY

Once clear on the mission, invest systematically in developing your people's ability to accomplish it. This includes:

- **Formal training in the skills the mission requires**: Don't just send people to training when convenient; rather, build capability development into the operational rhythm.
- **Challenging assignments that stretch people's abilities**: Give people responsibility slightly beyond their comfort zone, with appropriate support.
- **Mentoring and coaching**: Help people develop judgment and understanding, not just technical skills.
- **Cross-train**: So the team has depth and resilience, and will avoid single points of failure.

Every hour invested in developing people's capabilities is an hour invested in mission readiness. When my boss told me I needed to leave and gain CIO experience elsewhere, he was serving both the organization and me. He was helping me grow, which ultimately made the organization stronger.

REMOVE OBSTACLES

A huge part of serving people is removing obstacles that prevent them from doing their best work. This includes:

- **Bureaucratic nonsense**: Wastes time without adding value. Fight to eliminate or streamline processes that frustrate the team without serving the mission.

- **Resource shortfalls**: Forces people to work around inadequate tools or support. Advocate for what the team needs.
- **Unclear direction from above.** When higher leadership provides confusing or contradictory guidance, clarify it before it reaches the team.
- **Interpersonal conflicts**: These drain energy and create dysfunction. Address team dynamics before they become toxic.

Your people should be spending their energy on mission-relevant work, not fighting through obstacles that could be removed. When their path is clear, the mission is enabled.

MAKE DECISIONS WITH BOTH MISSION AND PEOPLE IN MIND

Every significant decision should be evaluated through two lenses:

- **How does this serve the mission?** If a choice doesn't advance objectives, why are you making it?
- **How does this affect my people?** What's the impact on their capability, morale, development, and well-being?

Sometimes these considerations align perfectly. You implement a new training program that both improves mission readiness and develops people's skills. Easy decision.

Sometimes there's tension. You need to deploy people on a demanding project that will require long hours and high stress. How do you decide?

This is where the *mission first, people always* principle provides clarity. If the mission genuinely requires the effort, move forward, but do everything possible to take care of your people in the process.

Ensure they have the resources they need. Rotate people to prevent burnout. Recognize and appreciate their sacrifice. Build in recovery time afterward.

What you don't do is demand unnecessary sacrifice. Don't create hardship through poor planning and then call it "mission first." Don't treat people as expendable because there's always someone else you can hire.

COMMUNICATE CONSTANTLY

A team needs to hear, repeatedly, that both the mission and their well-being matter to you. Don't assume they know. *Tell them*:

- **When making a difficult decision**: Explain your reasoning. Help them see how you're balancing mission requirements with people considerations.
- **When someone is sacrificing for the mission**: Acknowledge it. Make sure they know you see their effort and appreciate it.
- **When investing in someone's development**: Explain why. Help them understand that you're committed to their growth, not just extracting value from them.

Communication isn't about being soft or making people feel good. It's about ensuring everyone understands the reality you're operating in and the values guiding your decisions.

The Long View

Mission first, people always isn't a short-term tactic. It's a long-term philosophy that compounds over time.

In the short term, you can sometimes extract high performance by pushing people hard and ignoring their needs. But this approach burns people out, drives away the best performers, and ultimately degrades capability.

Over the long term, leaders who genuinely care for their people, while also maintaining focus on the mission, build organizations that are more capable, resilient, and successful.

When I returned to my original school district as CIO—the job I had aspired to years before—I inherited a team that my predecessor had built with this philosophy. He had invested in people's development. The result was a department that functioned at a high level and attracted talented people who wanted to work there.

My job was to continue that legacy. To maintain the balance and keep the mission front and center while ensuring every team member knew they mattered. I was able to increase the investment in people, even for those beyond my department.

THE FALSE CHOICE BETWEEN MISSION AND PEOPLE

One of the most damaging misconceptions in leadership is that you must choose between being mission-focused and people-focused. This false dichotomy creates terrible leaders on both extremes.

The Mission Tyrant

On one end, there are leaders who are mission-obsessed at the expense of everything else. They drive people relentlessly, ignore individual needs, and treat team members as disposable resources. They justify their approach by claiming that "the mission comes first" and "this isn't a social club."

These leaders often achieve short-term results. They can push people hard enough to hit immediate targets. But they create long-term damage:

- They burn people out, degrading future capability.
- They drive away talented people who have other options.
- They create environments where people hide problems rather than solve them.
- They miss opportunities for innovation because people are too demoralized to suggest improvements.
- They build teams that perform only under direct supervision because there's no genuine commitment.

Ironically, mission tyrants ultimately fail at mission accomplishment. They may hit this quarter's targets, but they degrade the organization's long-term capability.

The People Pleaser

On the other extreme, there are leaders who are so focused on keeping people happy that they lose sight of the mission. They avoid difficult decisions, maintain low standards, and prioritize comfort over capability.

These leaders are often well-liked initially. People appreciate not being pushed hard. But over time, problems emerge:

- The team's capability stagnates because there's no pressure to grow.
- Mission performance suffers because standards are too low.
- The best performers become frustrated because excellence isn't valued.

- The organization loses credibility with stakeholders and customers.
- Eventually, external pressure forces change, often traumatically.

People pleasers also ultimately fail. They may maintain good relationships, but they don't build the capable, high-performing teams that both accomplish the mission and provide meaningful work.

The Integrated Approach

The leaders who succeed long-term reject the false-choice dilemma. They understand that mission and people aren't competing values; they're complementary dimensions of the same responsibility. Such leaders:

- Maintain high standards while investing in people's ability to meet them.
- Push people to grow while providing the support and resources they need.
- Demand excellence while recognizing that it requires capable, committed people.
- Focus intensely on results while understanding that sustainable results require sustainable practices.
- Care deeply about both what gets accomplished and how it gets accomplished.

This integrated approach is harder than either extreme. It requires more judgment, more attention, and more nuance. You can't just default to "push harder" or "keep everyone happy." You have to think.

But it's also more effective. Leaders who successfully integrate mission focus with genuine care for people build organizations that perform at a high level year after year.

The Compounding Effect

Here's what makes mission first, people so powerful; it compounds over time.

When investing in people's capability, they become more effective. The increased effectiveness makes mission accomplishment easier. Success builds confidence and commitment, which leads to more discretionary effort. That extra effort leads to better results and more opportunities. Those opportunities attract better people and provide more room for development. The cycle reinforces itself.

Over months and years, this compounding effect creates organizations that are dramatically more capable than those led with either mission tyranny or people-pleasing.

I saw this with the boss who told me I needed to leave and gain experience elsewhere. He could have just kept me in place. I was doing good work, and replacing me would be inconvenient. But he invested in my development. That investment paid dividends for both of us; I gained the capability I needed, and the district eventually got a more capable leader back.

When I became CIO, I tried to create that same environment for my team. The compounding effect was remarkable. As people grew more capable, we could tackle more ambitious projects. As we succeeded at those, we gained more resources and opportunities. As we gained recognition, we attracted talented people who wanted to work with us. Each success made the next one more achievable.

That's the long-term power of genuinely integrating mission focus with people development.

COMMON MISTAKES TO AVOID

When integrating *mission first, people always* into your leadership skillset, watch out for the following common pitfalls.

Talking Mission, Acting People-Pleasing

Some leaders understand mission first intellectually but can't bring themselves to make the necessary hard decisions. They maintain low standards because raising them would be uncomfortable. They avoid difficult conversations because they don't want conflict. They say the mission matters, but act as though avoiding discomfort matters more.

This approach fails both the mission and your people. The mission suffers from low performance, and your team doesn't develop because they're not being pushed to grow.

- **The Fix**: Remember that maintaining high standards and having difficult conversations are ways of serving your people, not just serving the mission. You're not doing anyone a favor by accepting mediocrity.

Confusing Mission with Personal Ambition

Some leaders convince themselves that their personal career advancement serves the mission. They push for high-profile projects that look good on their resume but don't actually serve the organization's core objectives. They drive their teams hard to hit metrics that matter to their performance review, but not to the actual mission.

This approach uses both the mission and people as instruments of personal ambition rather than serving either one genuinely.

- **The Fix**: Regularly ask whose interests are really being served by your decision-making. Are you pursuing what the organization needs or what advances your career? These sometimes align, but not always.

Sacrificing People for Self-Inflicted Mission Crises

Some leaders create urgency through poor planning, then demand that their team sacrifice to meet artificial deadlines. They fail to prepare adequately, then ask people to work weekends. They don't address problems early, then create crises that require heroic effort.

This approach treats people badly while claiming mission necessity, when the real problem is leadership failure.

- **The Fix**: Distinguish between genuine mission requirements and consequences of poor planning. When you create the crisis, own it. Don't ask the team to pay the price for your mistakes without acknowledging your role.

Treating All Mission Requirements as Equally Urgent

Some leaders operate in constant crisis mode. Everything is urgent. Every request from above is treated as an emergency. The team is always in high-intensity mode.

This burns people out and actually undermines mission accomplishment by preventing thoughtful work and a sustainable pace.

- **The Fix**: Develop better judgment about what genuinely requires immediate action versus what can wait. Protect your team from artificial urgency while ensuring they understand and respond to real priorities.

INTEGRATION, NOT BALANCE

I want to address one final point about the language we use. People often talk about "work-life balance" or "balancing mission and people." But balance implies a trade-off; more of one means less of the other.

That's not how *mission first, people always* works.

It's about integration, not balance. Attention isn't separated between mission and people. It is recognized that everything you do as a leader has both mission and people dimensions.

- **When planning a project**: Think about both what needs to be accomplished and how to structure the work so your people can be successful.
- **When developing someone's capabilities**: Think about both their growth and how their increased capability serves the mission.
- **When making resource decisions**: Think about both mission requirements and people's needs.

It's not a seesaw action where the mission goes up when people go down. It's a reinforcing system; serving one will serve the other.

Such integration becomes more natural over time. Initially, you might have to consciously remind yourself to consider both dimensions. Eventually, it becomes instinctive. You automatically evaluate decisions through both lenses.

That's when you've truly internalized *mission first, people always*.

While reading, keep coming back to this question: "How does this principle help me serve both the mission and my people?"

That question will guide you toward better leadership decisions, stronger team performance, and more sustainable success.

REAL-WORLD SCENARIO: THE STRUGGLING TEAM MEMBER

I had a technician, I'll call him John, who had been with my organization for several years. He was technically competent but had become increasingly unreliable. He was often late, made careless mistakes, and missed work.

From a pure mission perspective, John was becoming a liability. His mistakes created extra work for others. His unreliability meant we couldn't depend on him for critical tasks. Other team members were starting to resent covering for him. The easy solution was to document his performance issues and move toward termination.

But from a people perspective, something was clearly wrong. This wasn't who John had been. Something had changed.

I sat down with John privately and had a direct but caring conversation. I laid out specifically what I was observing, not as accusations, but as facts. Then I asked what was going on.

It turned out John was burned out with little hope that things would change. He also did not fully understand expectations and how his actions impacted the team.

Once I understood the situation more fully, we developed a plan together. John wanted to do good work, but he didn't always feel supported. We moved him to a team that was a better fit and where he felt more supported. And we set clear expectations about work, performance, and communication. If he was struggling, he was expected to tell me rather than just trying to power through.

John's performance improved significantly over the next few months; he had the support he needed. He remained a valuable team member for years afterward. And the entire team saw that when someone was struggling, we tried to help them rather than just cutting them loose.

- **The lesson**: Taking care of people isn't just about being nice; it's about understanding that life happens, and helping people through difficult periods preserves both their capability and the team's culture. The mission is better served by supporting people through challenges than by treating them as disposable.

Application

When reflecting on your leadership history, consider these questions:

- **Is your mission clear?** Can everyone on the team articulate what you're trying to accomplish and why it matters?
- **Are you investing in people's capability?** What have you done in the past month to develop team members' skills, knowledge, or judgment?
- **Are you removing obstacles?** What unnecessary barriers are preventing people from doing their best work?
- **How do you make difficult decisions?** When mission and people considerations create tension, how do you think through the integration?
- **What does your communication reveal about your priorities?** If someone listened to what you talk about most often, would they conclude that both mission and people matter to you?

Mission first, people always isn't a formula that solves every leadership challenge. It's a lens through which to view your responsibilities. It reminds you to take accountability for both accomplishing the organization's objectives and developing the people who make success possible.

Your mission matters. Your people matter. Your job is to honor both, every single day.

DAILY PRACTICES

Understanding *mission first, people always* conceptually is valuable. But leadership is about action, not just understanding. How do you actually implement this philosophy in daily leadership practices?

- **Start the day with mission clarity**: Before getting pulled into the urgent tasks and emails, remember what you're trying to accomplish. What's the team's mission? What are your priorities? This clarity should inform every decision you make.
- **End the day with people reflection**: Before leaving work, think about your interactions with team members. Did anyone need support you didn't provide? Is anyone showing signs of struggle? Who did something worth recognizing? This reflection keeps people front of mind.
- **Ask better questions in meetings**: Instead of just reviewing status, ask questions that reveal both mission progress and people's health:

    - **What's blocking your progress?** Removes obstacles.
    - **What would help you be more effective?** Serves people's needs.
    - **What risks are we not seeing?** Surfaces problems early.
    - **Who needs recognition for their contribution?** Values people.

- **Make time for development conversations.** Schedule regular one-on-ones with team members that aren't just about current task status. Talk about their growth, their aspirations, and how you can help them develop.

WEEKLY PRACTICES

- **Review resource allocation**: Are you investing in capability building, or just consuming current capacity? Are there training needs that should be addressed? Equipment or tools that would make the team more effective?
- **Assess team health**: Beyond just task completion, how is the team functioning? Is morale good? Are relationships healthy? Is anyone showing signs of burnout or disengagement?
- **Celebrate progress**: Take time to recognize what the team has accomplished, both in mission and in individual growth terms. People need to see that their efforts matter.

MONTHLY PRACTICES

- **Evaluate balance**: Are you actually living *mission first, people always*, or have you drifted toward one extreme? Look at how you spend time and what you talk about the most. Does it reflect both mission and people priorities?
- **Solicit feedback**: Ask the team how you're doing. Are they getting what they need? Do they feel supported? Is the mission clear? You can't improve what you don't know about.

- **Plan for development:** What capabilities will the team need in the future? Who's ready for new challenges? Where should you invest in training or growth opportunities?

The Leadership Foundation

Everything else in this book builds on the foundation of *mission first, people always.* As I explore specific leadership practices in subsequent chapters—developing leaders at all levels, making decisions under pressure, building trust, creating accountability, communicating effectively, adapting to change, and building lasting legacies—they will all rest on this core principle.

Mission first, people always.
Not mission first, people second.
Not mission or people, choose one.
Mission first, people always.
Both. Simultaneously. Inseparably.
That's the foundation of effective leadership.

Chapter 2

Lead by Example: Actions Over Words

The first time I truly understood the power of leading by example, I wasn't the one doing the leading; I was watching it fail spectacularly.

We had experienced a set of military leaders who led by example. They never gave speeches about standards. Instead, they showed up early for formation every day. They led from the front on runs and regularly smoked soldiers half their age on the PT test. When we had a soldier who wasn't meeting the standard, we all did the work together to help that soldier get better. Their equipment was immaculate. In the field, they were always where the work was hardest, and the conditions were the worst.

They didn't have to tell us what the standard was. We could see it. And because we could see it, we wanted to meet it.

As with all units, those leaders rotated out, and we had a new sergeant who arrived with an impressive resume and a lot to say about standards. He talked about leadership, physical fitness, and discipline.

The speech was good. The follow-through was not.

Within a few weeks, we noticed he made decisions in his best interest. He would show up for unit runs but fade to the back and cut corners on the route. His equipment was serviceable but never exceeded the minimum standard. When we had hard work to do, he found reasons to be elsewhere.

His words said "excellence." His actions said "do as I say, not as I do."

The impact was immediate—and devastating. Soldiers who had been performing well began to slack off. "If the team sergeant doesn't have to do it, why should I?" became the unspoken sentiment. Standards eroded. Morale plummeted. The team's effectiveness suffered.

This is the essence of leading by example: actions speak so loudly that words become almost unnecessary.

The Military Standard: Leadership by Presence

In the military, particularly in the combat arms and special operations communities I served in, there's an unwritten but ironclad rule. Leaders never ask their people to do something they wouldn't do themselves.

This wasn't just about fairness or morale, though it affected both. It was about credibility and effectiveness. In environments where people might be asked to risk their lives, they need to know their leaders understand what they're asking. They need to see that their leaders share the hardships, the dangers, and the discomforts.

During my time in Iraq, I saw this principle tested daily. The work we did required us to have teams in some of the most dangerous areas of the country. Our Chaplain visited every team. He shared the risks, spent long hours in full combat gear under the Iraqi sun, and earned loyalty that went beyond the chain of command.

Our Sergeant Major, the senior enlisted leader in the unit, could have justified staying back to coordinate and plan. Instead, he went on every single convoy. When his soldiers asked him why, his answer was simple, "If I'm asking you to do it, I should be willing to do it first."

That sergeant major never had trouble getting his team to volunteer for difficult missions. They would have followed him anywhere.

THE CIVILIAN TRANSLATION: VISIBLE LEADERSHIP

When I transitioned to civilian technology leadership, I initially thought this principle might not apply as directly. After all, we weren't facing physical danger or asking people to risk their lives. But I quickly learned that leading by example is just as critical in the civilian world; it just looks different.

As a network technician, I watched my supervisors carefully. The ones who earned my respect and effort were the ones who didn't just manage from their desks. When there was a major outage and someone needed to crawl under a building to fix a cable, they were there. When we had to work late into the night for a critical system upgrade, they stayed until it was done. When there was a difficult conversation with an upset principal, they handled it rather than delegating the unpleasant task.

The supervisors who led by example never had trouble getting volunteers when something difficult needed to be done. The ones who delegated the hard work while keeping the comfortable tasks for themselves always struggled to build effective teams.

Early in my leadership career, I made a conscious decision to apply this principle systematically. If I expected my technicians to respond to after-hours emergencies, I made sure they saw me responding to them, too. If I wanted them to treat frustrated teachers with patience and respect, I modeled that behavior in every interaction. If I asked them to document their work thoroughly, I documented my own work to the same standard.

The impact was significant. When I later moved on to larger organizations, this foundation of credibility made it much easier to lead through change and challenge. My team knew that I wouldn't ask them to do anything I wasn't willing to do myself.

THE SERVANT LEADERSHIP CONNECTION: EXAMPLE AS SERVICE

Leading by example isn't just a military principle; it's a core tenet of servant leadership as well. Servant leadership begins with the natural feeling that one wants to serve. Leading by example is one of the most powerful ways to serve your team:

- **When modeling excellence**: You're serving the team by showing them what's possible.
- **When demonstrating integrity**: You're serving them by creating an environment of trust.
- **When handling adversity with grace**: You're serving them by teaching them how to be resilient.
- **When admitting mistakes**: You're serving them by making it safe to be human and imperfect.

As a CIO, my ultimate purpose was to serve the educational mission of the organization. My team's purpose was the same. When I modeled servant leadership—when my team saw me prioritizing the needs of teachers and students, handling difficult situations with patience and grace, and working to understand problems before jumping to solutions—I wasn't just leading by example. I was serving them by showing them what servant leadership looked like in practice.

One particular incident stands out. We had a major network outage right before payroll was due, the worst possible timing. School staff were frustrated, and the payroll department was especially stressed. I could have stayed in my office managing the crisis from a distance, directing my team while I handled communications with administration.

Instead, I grabbed a laptop and set up some hotspots for our team and went to work. Not because I was the best person to fix the technical problem, but because my team needed to see that we were all in this together, that I wasn't above doing the hard work, and that serving the schools meant being present in the difficult moments, not just the easy ones.

We fixed the problem and got the payroll office connected. But more importantly, my team learned something about leadership that day—that the CIO's job wasn't to be above the fray, but to enable the work and, when necessary, be in the work. That lesson influenced how they led their own teams and interacted with the teachers and staff they served.

The Five Dimensions of Leading by Example

Leading by example isn't just about work ethic or physical presence. It operates across multiple dimensions, each critical to building credibility and inspiring your team.

WORK STANDARDS

The most obvious dimension is the quality and quantity of work. If the expectation is for the team to produce high-quality work, your work must meet or exceed that standard. If you expect them to work hard, they need to see you working hard.

This doesn't mean doing the same work they do; they understand that the leadership role is different. But it means your work, whatever it is, reflects the same standards expected of them.

TREATMENT OF OTHERS

How you treat people, especially people who can't do anything for you, speaks volumes about your character and values.

A team watches how leaders treat the custodian, the receptionist, the vendor who made a mistake, and the employee who's struggling. If you preach respect and teamwork but treat support staff dismissively, your words become meaningless. Talk about developing people, but lose patience with someone who's learning, then the commitment to development rings hollow.

I learned this lesson powerfully during my time as a company commander for a Basic Training unit. The drill sergeants and I had enormous power over the trainees. How we exercised that power, especially when no one was watching, defined who we were as leaders.

The drill sergeants who commanded the most genuine respect were the ones who were tough but fair, who maintained standards without being cruel, who corrected mistakes without humiliating people. The ones who belittled soldiers or enjoyed their power too much might have been feared, but they weren't respected, and they weren't effective at developing soldiers who could think and lead on their own.

In the civilian world, this dimension of leadership is just as important.

HANDLING ADVERSITY

Anyone can lead when things are going well. The true test of leadership, and the moments when your example matters most, comes when things go wrong.

Stay calm under pressure, or panic? Own mistakes, or deflect blame? Work to solve problems, or waste energy complaining about them? Support the team when they're under fire, or throw them under the bus?

Your team watches closely during the difficult times. How you handle adversity sets the tone for how they'll handle it.

Throughout my career, I saw both ends of this spectrum. Some leaders became better versions of themselves under pressure, calmer, more focused, more decisive. Others fell apart, became angry and unpredictable, or retreated into blame and excuse-making.

The leaders who modeled grace under pressure built teams that could handle anything. The leaders who fell apart built teams that became anxious and ineffective when challenges arose.

One of my most powerful learning experiences came when I was laid off from the software company, a blow to my confidence and my sense of identity. I struggled. But that period taught me something valuable about resilience and humility, which made me a better leader later.

When I eventually led large teams, and someone was going through a difficult time, whether professional or personal, I could draw on that experience and model that setbacks aren't failures, that struggle is part of growth, and that asking for help is a sign of strength, not weakness.

CONTINUOUS IMPROVEMENT

If you expect the team to grow and develop, they need to see you growing and developing.

This was one of the most important lessons from my own career progression. When my boss gave me honest feedback about advancing to his role as CIO, that I needed to get broader experience and formal education, I could have been defensive or resentful. Instead, I took his advice.

I went back to school and earned my bachelor's in Business while working full-time. Later, I started my MBA. I actively sought opportunities to expand my skills and experience. Others saw me doing the work, studying, learning, and taking on new challenges.

That visible commitment to development gave me credibility when I encouraged them to pursue their own growth. When I asked a technician to learn a new system or pursue a certification, I wasn't asking them to do something I wasn't doing myself.

INTEGRITY AND CONSISTENCY

Perhaps the most critical dimension of leading by example is integrity, the alignment between what you say and what you do, and the consistency of your behavior over time.

Integrity means following the same rules you expect others to follow. It means being the same person whether people are watching or not.

Consistency means the team can predict how you'll respond. They know what you value because your actions consistently reflect those values. They trust you because your behavior doesn't change due to mood or circumstances.

In special operations, integrity and consistency weren't optional. Lives depended on trust. If a team couldn't trust its leader to do what he said he would do, the team couldn't function. Our high-performing teams in Iraq were built on the foundation of leaders whose word was absolutely reliable. I saw leaders sent home when they didn't meet that standard.

In civilian leadership, the stakes are usually less dramatic, but the principle remains crucial. When a team knows they can count on a leader to keep their commitments, to treat them fairly regardless of mood, and to apply standards consistently, they can focus on the work rather than managing their relationship with their boss.

The Practical Challenges: When Leading by Example Is Difficult

Leading by example sounds straightforward, but in practice, it can be challenging. Let's address some common difficulties.

DIFFERENT ROLES, DIFFERENT RESPONSIBILITIES

Responsibilities diverge from the team's as you advance up the leadership ladder. So, how do you lead by example when you're not doing the same work?

The answer is to focus on universal behaviors rather than specific tasks. Maybe you don't troubleshoot network issues anymore, but you can still demonstrate:

- Thoroughness in your work.
- Responsiveness to requests.
- Respect in your interactions.
- Accountability for decisions.
- Commitment to continuous learning.
- Balance between mission and people.

Such behaviors transcend specific roles and are relevant regardless of what job you're doing.

When I became a company commander, I wasn't doing the work of an NCO anymore. But I could still demonstrate what right looked like: showing up prepared, treating soldiers with firm respect, maintaining standards, being present in difficult moments, and owning my decisions.

THE VISIBILITY PROBLEM

Some leadership work happens behind closed doors. Negotiating budgets, having personnel discussions, managing up to superiors, and dealing with sensitive issues. The team can't see that work, so how can you lead by example with it?

The solution is strategic transparency. Much can't be shared, but enough can be so that the team understands how you approach your responsibilities. After difficult meetings or decisions, I often share (appropriately) with my team:

- Here's what I was wrestling with.
- Here's how I thought through it.
- Here's why I made the decision I made.

Doing so provides insight into my decision-making process and values, even though they couldn't observe the work directly.

I also made sure that the work they could see—emails, presentations, interactions, meetings—reflected the same standards and values as the work they couldn't see.

WORK-LIFE BALANCE

Leading by example can feel like it requires sacrificing your personal life. If you're always having to demonstrate work ethic, when do you take care of yourself and your family?

This is a critical tension. The answer is that leading by example includes modeling healthy boundaries and self-care. If you burn out, you're not helping anyone. If your family suffers because you're always at work, you're not demonstrating the values of balance and priorities that you should want your team to embrace.

I learned this lesson the hard way. Early in my civilian leadership career, I fell into the trap of trying to work harder than anyone, to always be available, to never say no. I thought I was leading by example. Instead, I was modeling unsustainable behavior and setting an unrealistic expectation. I was also sacrificing important time with my family.

After helping a customer on short notice, on a holiday weekend, I had an epiphany. I asked myself, "What are you doing? Does leadership mean sacrificing your health and family?"

It was a wake-up call. I started enforcing better boundaries. I would leave at reasonable times when there wasn't a genuine crisis. I would talk openly about attending my kids' events. I would take vacations. And I discovered something important. My team's respect didn't diminish. If anything, it increased, because they saw me modeling sustainable excellence rather than unsustainable "heroics."

THE AUTHENTICITY TRAP

Trying too hard to lead by example can seem inauthentic. Being watched becomes the focus; you end up performing, not genuinely leading.

The solution is to focus on becoming the person who naturally demonstrates the behaviors you want to model rather than constantly self-monitoring performance. This is about character development, not behavior management.

Instead of thinking "I need to appear patient in this situation because my team is watching," work on actually becoming more patient. Instead of "I need to appear to care about this person," work on genuinely caring.

This is harder but more sustainable. It's the difference between acting like a good leader and being a good leader. Over time, authentic character wins every time.

Common Pitfalls: When Leading by Example Goes Wrong

While leading by example is powerful, it's possible to do it wrong. Here are the most common pitfalls.

THE SUPERHERO SYNDROME

Some leaders try to lead by being better than everyone at everything. They work longer hours than anyone else, they excel at every task, and they never show weakness or admit mistakes.

This approach backfires. Instead of inspiring the team, it intimidates them or makes them feel inadequate. It also creates an unsustainable standard; the leader eventually burns out, or the team decides they can never measure up, so why try?

Leading by example doesn't mean being superhuman. It means being authentically excellent while also being human. It means working hard but also taking care of yourself. It means excelling in your areas of strength while acknowledging areas where others are better than you.

THE MICROMANAGER

Some leaders confuse leading by example with doing the work themselves. They jump in to handle every task, demonstrating the "right way" constantly, never trusting their team to figure things out. Never allowing others to do work in their own way.

This isn't leading by example; it's micromanaging. Leading by example means demonstrating standards and behaviors, then trusting the team to meet those standards in their own way. It means showing what right looks like without doing all the work yourself.

THE PERFORMATIVE LEADER

Some leaders put on a show of leading by example when people are watching, but behave differently when they're not. They make sure to be seen working hard, treating people well, and upholding standards, but in private or with their peers, they drop the act.

This eventually is discovered, and when it is, the damage to credibility is severe. Authentic leadership by example isn't about performance.

Actions Speak Louder

Words are easy; actions are hard. That's why actions carry so much more weight.

Anyone can talk about standards, values, and expectations. But living them—consistently, visibly, authentically—requires discipline, humility, and commitment.

When committed to leading by example, you're committing to being constantly watched and evaluated. That can feel uncomfortable. But it's also the source of your greatest influence.

A team doesn't need you to be perfect.

- They need you to be genuine.
- They need to see that you hold yourself to the same standards you expect from them.

- They need to know that you wouldn't ask them to do something you wouldn't do yourself.
- They need to watch you handle adversity, mistakes, and challenges with the same grace and accountability you expect from them.

When they see that—when your actions consistently align with your words—trust grows, respect deepens, and performance improves. Not because you demanded it, but because you demonstrated what excellence looks like, and the team chose to rise to that standard.

Your actions tomorrow will speak louder than any words you say today. Make sure they're saying what you want them to say.

THE COMPOUNDING EFFECT

The power of leading by example compounds over time. Each instance where actions align with words makes the next instance more powerful. Each time integrity is demonstrated, it builds credibility that makes your leadership more effective.

Conversely, each instance where actions contradict words erodes trust. Erosion happens much faster than the building. One significant failure to lead by example can undo months of consistent behavior.

I saw this dynamic clearly in one organization I led. We had a manager who was generally effective and well-respected. He talked about teamwork and trusting people to do their work. However, his employees came to find that he was not very flexible or trusting, and wanted things done only his way. He went beyond simple supervision and checked every detail. He didn't lead by example; he led by controlling everything to the smallest detail.

LEADING UP THROUGH EXAMPLE

Leadership above you is watching too. When you consistently demonstrate excellence, integrity, and the integration of mission focus with genuine care for people, you're influencing how leadership is perceived and practiced at levels above you.

During my time as a CIO, I reported to superintendents who had their own leadership styles and approaches. I couldn't change how they led, but I could model an alternative approach. When they saw the results—high performance combined with high morale, innovation combined with stability, efficiency combined with humanity—it influenced how they thought about my leadership.

Several times, superintendents I worked with changed their minds about practices they saw working in my department. Not because I told them they should, but because they saw the results and didn't want to disrupt the success we were having.

You lead "up" by manifesting the kind of leadership you wish your leaders would embrace.

LEADING ACROSS THROUGH EXAMPLE

Peers in other departments or organizations are watching too. When it's demonstrated that excellence and humanity can coexist, that mission focus and people focus aren't competing priorities, that servant leadership isn't soft leadership, you're influencing how leadership is understood across the entire organization.

I saw this dynamic repeatedly in organizations where I led and served. When the technology department consistently delivered excellent results while maintaining a positive, development-focused culture, other departments took notice.

Your example creates possibilities for others. It shows what's achievable when leadership principles are applied consistently.

The Long-Term Legacy

Perhaps most importantly, the people you lead today will be leaders themselves tomorrow. The example you set shapes not just their current performance but their future leadership.

I think about the drill sergeants who trained me, the NCOs I served under, the officers who commanded me. I carry their examples, both positive and negative, with me. When I face a leadership challenge, I often find myself thinking, "What would Sergeant Major do in this situation?" or "How would the captain handle this?"

The leaders who shaped me continue to influence the next generation through me. And the example I set continues through the people I've led who are now leading others. This is the ultimate multiplication of leadership. Your example, lived consistently over time, shapes leaders who shape other leaders who will shape still others. Influence extends across time and distance in ways you'll never fully see or measure. But it's real, and it matters. And it makes leading by example one of the most important investments you can make in the future of leadership itself.

THE ULTIMATE TEST: WHAT WOULD THEY SAY?

Here's the ultimate test of whether you're leading by example effectively:

- If your team members were asked to describe what leadership looks like based solely on watching you, what would they say?
- Would they describe a leader who works hard and expects others to work hard? Or a leader who tells others to work hard while taking it easy?

- Would they describe a leader who treats everyone with respect? Or a leader who's respectful to superiors but dismissive to peers and subordinates?
- Would they describe a leader who owns mistakes and learns from them? Or a leader who blames others and makes excuses?
- Would they describe a leader who serves the mission and the people? Or a leader who serves themselves?

The answers to these questions tell you everything you need to know about how well you're leading by example.

And a key insight is that your team is already answering these questions. They're watching you every day and forming conclusions about leadership based on what they see. The only question is whether you're intentional about what they're learning.

Practical Application: Building Your Example

Leading by example starts with a simple commitment: Tomorrow, your actions will align with your words.

You don't have to be perfect. You don't have to be the best at everything. You just have to be authentic about what you value and consistent in demonstrating those values through your behavior. Ask yourself:

- What behavior or quality do I most want to see in my team?
- Am I exemplifying that behavior or quality myself?
- Where are the gaps between what I say and what I do?
- What one change could I make tomorrow to better lead by example?

Your team is watching. They're always watching. Not because they're waiting for you to fail, but because they're looking for someone worth following.

Be that someone.

- Not through words, but through actions.
- Not through perfection, but through consistency.
- Not through performance, but through authenticity.

Lead by example, and watch your team rise to meet the standard you set.

Your actions speak. Make sure they're saying what you want them to say.

HOW TO SYSTEMATICALLY LEAD BY EXAMPLE

Here are practical strategies:

Identify the Behaviors That Matter Most

You can't be exemplary in every possible behavior, so focus on the ones that matter most for your team's success and culture.

What behaviors or qualities are most critical in your organization?

- Work ethic?
- Technical excellence?
- Customer service?
- Innovation?
- Collaboration?
- Integrity?

Make a list of the three to five behaviors or qualities that are most important, then ruthlessly examine whether your own behavior exemplifies them.

Make Your Work Visible

Leading by example only works if people can see the example. You don't need to be performative about it, but you do need to make sure your team has visibility into how you work and what you prioritize.

This might mean working in common areas sometimes instead of always behind closed doors. It might mean talking openly about challenges you're facing and how you're approaching them. It might mean including team members in activities where they can observe your leadership in action.

When I managed the technology department, I made a point of being present and visible. I didn't hide in my office. I visited technicians in schools. I walked through the workspace, attended team meetings, and made sure people saw me doing the work, not just directing it.

Acknowledge Mistakes Quickly

One of the most powerful ways to lead by example is to demonstrate how to handle mistakes well. When you mess up, acknowledge it quickly, take responsibility, fix what you can, and learn from it.

This models the behavior you want from the team. It shows that, if handled well, mistakes aren't career-ending events. It creates a culture where people can be honest about problems instead of hiding them.

Ask for Feedback

One of the most powerful questions you can ask is, "Do you see any gaps between what I say I value and how I actually behave?"

This requires humility and genuine openness to criticism. But it's also one of the best ways to identify blind spots where you might not be leading by example as effectively as you think.

Putting It into Practice: A 30-Day Challenge

Let me give you a practical framework for strengthening your leadership by example over the next thirty days.

DAYS 1–7: ASSESSMENT

- Identify the three behaviors or qualities most critical to your team's success.
- Honestly assess how well you currently demonstrate each one.
- Ask a trusted colleague or team member for feedback on gaps between your words and actions.
- Journal daily to answer questions like, "Where did my actions align with my values today? Where didn't they?"

DAYS 8–14: FOCUS ON ONE BEHAVIOR

- Choose one behavior to focus on intensively.
- Before each interaction or task, ask, "How would the person I want to be handle this?"
- Make your work in this area visible to the team.
- Share a story from your past that illustrates this behavior.

DAYS 15–21: DEMONSTRATE HANDLING ADVERSITY

- Identify a current challenge or problem.
- Handle it in a way that demonstrates your values: calm, accountable, solution-focused.
- Be transparent with the team about how you're approaching it.
- When something goes wrong (it will), own it quickly and completely.

DAYS 22–28: SHOW VULNERABILITY AND GROWTH

- Admit a mistake to the team and share what you learned.
- Ask for feedback on your leadership.
- Share something you're working on to improve yourself.
- Acknowledge an area where a team member has strengths you don't.

DAYS 29–30: REFLECT AND COMMIT

- Review your journal from the past month.
- Identify patterns: What's working? What's still challenging?
- Make a specific commitment about how you'll continue leading by example.
- Share your commitment with someone who will hold you accountable.

This isn't about perfection. It's about intentional, visible progress in becoming the leader your team deserves.

Chapter 3

Empower and Trust: Decentralized Leadership

The success of operations doesn't depend on a leader's ability to micromanage every action. It depends on whether a team is properly trained and empowered to make sound decisions in a leader's absence.

That is the essence of decentralized leadership, a principle I first encountered with the 82nd Airborne, and then saw perfected in Special Operations. It's the philosophy that won wars, like enabling success in Normandy, and continues to define effective military operations today. But more importantly, it's a leadership approach that transforms civilian organizations just as powerfully as it does military units.

Decentralized leadership is built on a profound act of trust, the belief that well-trained, well-equipped people closest to a problem are best positioned to solve it. This chapter explores how leaders can create organizations where initiative flourishes, decisions happen at the appropriate level, and people feel genuinely empowered to lead within their scope of responsibility.

The Military Foundation: A Commander's Intent and Mission Command

In military doctrine, particularly as practiced in the 1990s before over-bureaucratization set in, we operated under a concept called "mission command" or "commander's intent." The idea was elegantly simple. Leaders at every level needed to understand not just what to do, but why they were doing it, and what end state they were trying to achieve.

When I served with the 82nd Airborne, this principle was drilled into us constantly. Before any operation, the commander would clearly articulate intent—the purpose behind the mission and the desired outcome. The specific tactics of how to achieve outcomes were often left to subordinate leaders to determine based on the situation they encountered.

This approach acknowledged the fundamental truth that the person on the ground has information the person in the rear doesn't. Time-sensitive decisions can't always await approval from higher headquarters. Opportunities are missed, and dangers magnified, when every decision must flow up and down a chain of command.

THE LITTLE GROUPS PHILOSOPHY: EXCELLENCE THROUGH EMPOWERMENT

A good example of this trust-based approach is the Little Groups of Paratroopers (LGOPs) story from World War II's Normandy landing.

During the D-Day invasion, paratroopers from the 82nd and 101st Airborne were scattered across Normandy, often miles from their intended drop zones. Officers and NCOs found themselves separated from their units. The carefully planned operational structure dissolved in the chaos of combat.

What happened next defined a leadership philosophy. Small groups of soldiers, often led by junior NCOs or even privates, took initiative. They didn't wait for orders. They didn't freeze in uncertainty. They assessed their situation, identified what needed to be done to support the overall mission (which they understood), and they did it.

These LGOPs accomplished mission-critical objectives because they had been trained not just in technical skills, but in understanding the broader purpose of their operation. They knew why they were in Normandy. And they had been given permission, indeed, encouraged, to exercise judgment and initiative.

When I served with the 82nd Airborne decades later, this philosophy was still central to our culture. We were constantly reminded that "You might find yourself cut off, with no radio contact, leading soldiers who aren't from your unit. Can you still accomplish the mission?" The expected answer was yes, because we all understood the intent and had been empowered to act.

This same philosophy became critical when I transitioned to civilian leadership in the technology sector.

CIVILIAN APPLICATION: EMPOWERMENT

When I became the director of a department, I inherited a group that had been heavily centralized in its decision-making. Technicians waited for approval on routine matters. Staff escalated even minor issues. Projects stalled because everyone was waiting for direction from above them.

The organization wasn't suffering because people lacked competence. They were smart, skilled, and committed. It was failing because they had learned that taking initiative was risky. Previous leadership had created an environment where making a decision without approval could result in criticism, so people simply stopped making decisions.

I recognized this immediately from my military experience. This was the opposite of the LGOP philosophy. This was an organization where people had been trained to wait for orders rather than understand intent and execute.

My first priority was changing this culture, and I started by clearly articulating our department's intent. I brought the entire team together and laid out our mission in terms everyone could understand: "Our mission is to ensure that technology supports learning and never becomes a barrier to it. Every decision you make, every problem you solve, every project you undertake should be guided by this question: 'Does this support students first, then teachers, then everyone else?' If the answer is 'yes,' and it's within your area of responsibility, make it happen."

I also gave them permission to make mistakes within certain areas. I didn't want them to risk losing data or important information, but if they accidentally fried a motherboard, we used it as a learning experience.

This was met with skepticism at first. Years of working in a permission-based culture had created learned helplessness. People didn't trust that they really had the authority to act.

So, I reinforced the message with action. When a network technician made a decision to fix an issue during a crisis without asking me first, I publicly praised them for taking initiative. When a help desk specialist committed resources to solve a teacher's problem creatively, I backed the decision completely.

I also created clear boundaries. Empowerment doesn't mean chaos. Just as a military commander's intent provides both freedom and constraints, I defined areas where people had authority, areas where they should consult before acting, and areas reserved for executive decision-making. For example:

- **Full authority:** Troubleshooting and resolving technical issues, prioritizing support tickets based on impact to learning, and recommending solutions to recurring problems.
- **Consult before acting**: Expenditures over a certain threshold, or changes that might impact multiple buildings.
- **Executive decision**: Budget allocations, strategic technology direction, vendor contracts, organizational structure, decisions involving personnel matters.

This framework gave people the clarity they needed to act with confidence.

THE TRUST COMPONENT: EARNED AND GIVEN

Decentralized leadership requires trust flowing in both directions. As a leader, you must trust the team to make sound decisions. But your team must also trust that you'll support their decisions, even when those don't turn out perfectly.

This principle applied during my time leading in technology. I managed over seventy people and couldn't possibly be involved in every decision. I had to trust my managers to lead their teams, and they had to trust their team members to solve problems.

Training for Autonomy: Building Competence to Enable Empowerment

But trust isn't just given blindly; it's built on a foundation of competence and character. This is where training becomes essential.

You cannot empower people to make decisions if they lack the knowledge and skills to make those decisions well. Empowerment without competence creates chaos. This is why decentralized leadership requires significant investment in training and development.

In the military, we spent enormous amounts of time training for situations we might encounter. We rehearsed scenarios, discussed decision-making frameworks, and practiced until responses became second nature. This intensive preparation made decentralized execution possible.

We didn't just train on equipment and tactics.

- We trained in strategic thinking.
- We practiced analyzing situations from multiple perspectives.
- We studied cultural dynamics.
- We role-played difficult situations.
- We debated ethical dilemmas.

All of this prepared team members to make sound decisions independently when the situation demanded it.

I brought this same philosophy to civilian leadership. I established comprehensive training programs that went beyond technical skills.

We discussed scenarios in which technicians had to solve complex problems without a supervisor's input. We learned from other districts. We held regular professional development sessions.

Most importantly, I made sure every team member understood the broader context of our work. They didn't just know how to configure a network switch. They understood why network reliability mattered to student learning outcomes. They didn't just troubleshoot computers. They understood their role in ensuring equitable access to educational technology.

This contextual understanding transformed technical staff into educational technology professionals who could make strategic decisions, not just follow technical procedures.

CREATING SPACE FOR INITIATIVE: THE LEADER'S ROLE IN DECENTRALIZED ORGANIZATIONS

In a decentralized organization, the leader's role shifts significantly. You are not the primary decision-maker on most operational matters. So, what do you do?

- **Set and communicate clear intent**: You define what success looks like and why it matters. You paint the picture of the end state you're trying to achieve. You ensure everyone understands the mission and their role in accomplishing it.
- **Remove obstacles**: Teams will encounter barriers they can't remove themselves, like bureaucratic roadblocks, resource constraints, and conflicting priorities from other departments. Your job is to clear these obstacles so the team can execute. When I lead, I spend time running interference with other departments, advocating for resources, and navigating politics so my team can focus on their work without distraction.
- **Provide resources and support**: Empowerment requires equipping people with what they need to succeed, including training, tools, information, and authority. You ensure the team has the resources necessary to make good decisions and execute effectively.
- **Establish boundaries and guidelines**: Freedom without structure creates anxiety and inconsistency. You define the guardrails within which people can operate autonomously. This includes policies, budgets, ethical guidelines, and strategic priorities.
- **Coach and develop**: You help people grow in their decision-making capabilities. When someone makes a suboptimal decision, you don't punish them; you coach

them through better approaches. You use mistakes as teaching moments.

- **Protect your team**: When your team makes decisions within their authority, you support those decisions publicly, even if you might have chosen differently. You take responsibility for outcomes and shield your team from unfair criticism.
- **Recognize and celebrate initiative**: You make heroes of people who take appropriate initiative. You tell their stories. You reward problem-solving and creative thinking. You create a culture where taking smart risks is valued.

THE BOUNDARIES OF EMPOWERMENT: WHEN TO STEP IN

Decentralized leadership doesn't mean abdicating responsibility. There are times when leaders must step in and make direct decisions. Understanding when to intervene and when to let the team work through challenges is a critical leadership skill. I learned to step in when:

- **Safety is compromised**: If a decision puts people at risk, immediate intervention is necessary. This is nonnegotiable. In the military, we called this a "safety violation," and it stopped everything. The same principle applies in civilian organizations.
- **The decision exceeds the scope of authority**: If someone is making a decision that properly belongs at a higher level—major resource commitments, policy changes, strategic direction shifts—you need to redirect that decision to the appropriate level.
- **The team lacks critical information**: Sometimes, you have information that the team doesn't, which would

fundamentally change their decision. In such cases, you need to provide that information, though ideally, you're creating systems where information flows freely.

- **Patterns of poor judgment emerge**: If a team member consistently makes poor decisions despite coaching, you may need to narrow their decision-making authority while addressing the underlying competence or judgment issues.

But I learned ***not*** to step in when:

- **I would have done it differently**: If the team takes an approach distinct from mine, but which is still sound and within guidelines, I let them execute their way. Different doesn't mean wrong, and people learn best when they can apply their own judgment.
- **Short-term inefficiency is creating long-term learning**: Sometimes, the most efficient solution is for me to make the decision. But if letting the team work through the problem builds capability for the future, the short-term inefficiency is a worthwhile investment.
- **My intervention would undermine trust**: If stepping in would communicate, "I don't really trust you after all," the damage to the empowerment culture outweighs the benefit of my involvement.

MEASURING SUCCESS IN DECENTRALIZED ORGANIZATIONS

How do you know if decentralized leadership is working? Traditional metrics that focus on leader activity don't apply; you can't measure success by how many decisions you make if the goal is to make fewer decisions.

Instead, I learned to look for these indicators:

- **Operating velocity increases**: Problems get solved faster because people don't wait for permission. Opportunities are seized in real-time. The organization becomes more responsive.
- **Quality of decisions improves**: Because decisions are made by people closest to the problem with the most current information, the decisions tend to be better informed and more practical.
- **Innovation emerges**: When people feel empowered, they experiment with new approaches. They suggest improvements. They take ownership of outcomes in ways that generate creative solutions.
- **People grow in capability**: Team members develop stronger judgment, deeper understanding of the mission, and greater confidence in their abilities. You see leadership emerging at every level.
- **The leader becomes less critical**: The organization doesn't grind to a halt when you're unavailable. People continue to execute effectively in your absence. This is actually a sign of success, not irrelevance.

When I've left leadership positions, the programs and people continued to thrive without me. My successors have told me later that the transitions are often seamless because the teams are accustomed to operating with autonomy. They didn't need me to function, which meant I had succeeded in building a truly empowered organization.

COMMON PITFALLS AND HOW TO AVOID THEM

Implementing decentralized leadership isn't without challenges. I made plenty of mistakes along the way, and I've seen other leaders struggle with common pitfalls.

- **Empowerment without clarity**: Telling people "you're empowered" without clearly defining boundaries, expectations, and intent creates confusion, not initiative. People need to know what they're empowered to do and what success looks like.
    - **Solution**: Invest time in clearly communicating intent, defining scope of authority, and establishing decision-making frameworks. Put it in writing. Discuss it repeatedly. Make it crystal clear.
- **Inconsistent support**: Supporting decisions when they work out but second-guessing them when they don't destroys trust faster than never empowering people in the first place.
    - **Solution**: Commit to supporting decisions made in good faith within established guidelines, even when outcomes aren't perfect. Save critiques for private coaching conversations, not public undermining.
- **Empowering before training**: Pushing decisions down to people who aren't prepared to make them sets them up for failure and creates justified anxiety about taking initiative.
    - **Solution**: Build competence before expanding autonomy. Provide training, mentoring, and gradually increasing responsibility as people demonstrate capability.
- **Confusing empowerment with abandonment**: Some leaders think empowerment means stepping back com-

pletely and leaving people to figure everything out alone. This creates isolation, not independence.

  - **Solution**: Stay engaged through coaching, resource provision, obstacle removal, and regular communication. Be available without being controlling.

- **One-size-fits-all empowerment**: Different people and different situations require different levels of autonomy. Treating everyone identically ignores individual development levels and contextual factors.

  - **Solution**: Adjust empowerment levels based on individual competence, experience, and the specific situation. This isn't favoritism; it's appropriate leadership.

THE LONG-TERM IMPACT: ORGANIZATIONS THAT LEAD THEMSELVES

The ultimate goal of decentralized leadership is creating organizations that function effectively at every level, with leadership distributed rather than concentrated, and the absence of any single person, including you, is not a crisis.

This was the goal in military units I served with, and it's proven equally valuable in civilian organizations. When I've moved on, I've left behind teams that continued to excel because the culture of empowerment and initiative had become self-sustaining.

Similarly, when I took on a larger role, I built a leadership team that could manage day-to-day operations without my constant involvement. This freed me to focus on strategic initiatives, relationship building with other departments, and long-term planning.

It was all work that couldn't have happened if I were constantly consumed with operational decisions.

More importantly, it created an environment where talented people wanted to work and stay. People don't leave jobs where they feel trusted, empowered, and able to make a real difference. The retention and engagement levels in teams I led were consistently high because people felt genuine ownership of their work.

This is the servant leadership dimension of decentralized leadership. By empowering others, you serve their growth and development. By trusting them with real authority, you demonstrate respect for their capabilities. By stepping back from control, you create space for them to step into leadership.

THE COURAGE TO LET GO

Decentralized leadership requires courage. The courage to trust others with decisions that have real consequences, the courage to let go of control, and the courage to accept that sometimes people will make different choices than you would have made.

This courage is easier to summon when remembering that your role as a leader isn't being the smartest person in the room. Your role is to build an organization where excellence can flourish at every level, where initiative is the norm rather than the exception, and where people are equipped and empowered to lead within their scope of responsibility.

The LGOPs philosophy, which proved itself in Normandy, and which remained vital in my time with the 82nd Airborne, isn't just military nostalgia; it's a timeless leadership truth. Organizations succeed when people at every level understand the mission, feel trusted to contribute, and are empowered to act.

The Neuroscience of Empowerment: Why This Approach Works

While military and civilian experience demonstrates that decentralized leadership works, it's worth understanding why it's so effective. Modern neuroscience and organizational psychology provide compelling explanations.

AUTONOMY AS A CORE HUMAN NEED

Research consistently shows that autonomy—the feeling of having control over one's work and decisions—is one of the fundamental human psychological needs. When people feel they have genuine autonomy, several positive effects occur:

- Intrinsic motivation increases dramatically.
- Engagement and commitment to outcomes strengthen.
- Creativity and problem-solving improve.
- Stress and burnout decrease.
- Job satisfaction rises significantly.

Decentralized leadership directly satisfies this need for autonomy. When empowering people to make decisions within their scope of responsibility, you're not just being a nice leader; you're activating fundamental psychological drivers that improve performance.

Conversely, excessive control and micromanagement trigger psychological threat responses. People feel their autonomy is constrained, which reduces motivation, increases stress, and diminishes cognitive function. This is why centralized, controlling leadership often produces worse outcomes despite leaders' good intentions.

COGNITIVE LOAD AND DECISION QUALITY

Another factor is cognitive load. Every person has limited mental bandwidth. When leaders try to make every decision, they become bottlenecks not just in terms of time but in terms of cognitive capacity.

You simply cannot maintain a deep understanding of every situation across an organization. The people closest to each situation have information you don't have and contextual understanding you can't replicate from a distance.

When decisions flow to the people with the best information and deepest context, decision quality improves. This isn't theoretical; it's supported by extensive research on distributed decision-making in complex systems.

Cultural Considerations: Adapting Decentralization Across Contexts

While the principles of decentralized leadership are universal, the application must be culturally sensitive and context-appropriate. What works in a US military special operations unit may need adaptation for a civilian organization, a different cultural context, or a different industry.

During my time in Korea as an intelligence analyst, I learned that Korean military culture had different norms around hierarchy and decision-making than American military culture. What was seen as appropriate initiative in US units might be viewed as disrespectful in Korean units. Effective cross-cultural military operations required understanding and respecting these differences while still finding ways to enable effective decentralized execution.

Similarly, in civilian organizations, industry culture matters. A technology startup may embrace radical decentralization more easily than a highly regulated financial institution, where compliance requirements demand more structured decision processes.

The key is to adapt the principles to your context without abandoning them entirely. Even in highly hierarchical or regulated environments, you can still:

- Ensure people understand the why behind decisions, not just the what.
- Create space for input and initiative within appropriate boundaries.
- Develop people's judgment and decision-making capabilities.
- Push decisions to the lowest appropriate level given constraints.
- Trust people with genuine responsibility within their scope.

The goal isn't to eliminate all structure or hierarchy; it's to ensure that structure serves the mission rather than existing for its own sake.

The Learning Effect

Perhaps most importantly, decentralized leadership creates a continuous learning environment. When people make decisions and experience the consequences, both positive and negative, they develop judgment and expertise far more effectively than if they simply execute decisions made by others.

This is why decentralized organizations tend to develop deeper bench strength. Leadership capability isn't concentrated in a few individuals at the top; it's distributed throughout the organization. People at every level are practicing leadership skills, making judgment calls, and growing in competence.

When I left leadership positions, whether in the military or civilian world, I hoped the organizations continued to thrive because I had been developing leaders at every level, not just executing decisions from the top.

Building the System: Processes That Enable Decentralization

Effective decentralized leadership requires supporting systems and processes. You can't simply declare "everyone is empowered" and expect good outcomes. You need infrastructure that enables distributed decision-making while maintaining alignment.

INFORMATION SHARING SYSTEMS

Decentralized decision-making requires that information flows freely to the people who need it. In centralized organizations, information often concentrates at the top. Leaders know things that their teams don't, which creates information asymmetry that prevents effective distributed decision-making.

I established the following regular information-sharing practices in one organization:

- Weekly email updates on strategic initiatives and key decisions.
- Monthly all-staff meetings where we discussed challenges and direction.
- Shared dashboards showing key metrics and performance indicators.
- An open-door policy where anyone could ask questions about strategy or context.

- Collaborative planning processes where team input shaped direction.

This ensured that when my team members made decisions, they had the context and information necessary to make good choices aligned with organizational goals.

FEEDBACK LOOPS

Decentralized organizations need robust feedback mechanisms so learning happens continuously and decisions can be adjusted based on outcomes. For example:

- After-action reviews for significant projects or incidents.
- Regular one-on-ones that include decision-making and judgment development.
- Team discussions of challenges and solutions.
- Systems for sharing lessons learned across the organization.
- Metrics that show whether decentralized decisions were producing desired outcomes.

Such feedback loops ensure that empowerment leads to continuous improvement rather than repeated mistakes.

CLEAR ESCALATION PATHS

Even in decentralized organizations, people need to know when and how to escalate decisions that exceed their scope or require higher-level input. Clear escalation paths prevent both decision paralysis and inappropriate risk-taking.

Make sure everyone knows:

- What situations require escalation.
- How to escalate quickly when needed.
- That escalating appropriately is valued, not viewed as weakness.
- Who to contact for different types of decisions.
- What information to provide when escalating.

Clarity gives people confidence to act within their authority while also ensuring they get support when situations require it.

The Servant Leadership Connection: Empowerment as Service

Decentralized leadership is fundamentally an act of servant leadership. When empowering others, you serve their growth and development and demonstrate respect for their capabilities. Conditions are created for them to flourish and contribute their best work.

This requires humility, a recognition that you don't have to be the hero of every story. Your role is to enable others to be heroes in their own domains.

It also requires patience. Developing decentralized leadership capability takes time. People need to build confidence, develop judgment, and learn from experience. There will be mistakes along the way. The servant leader views this as an investment, not a cost.

One of the most rewarding aspects of my leadership journey has been watching people I empowered go on to significant leadership roles themselves. The specialist who learned to trust his judgment became an NCO. The technician who struggled previously improved and later became a team leader. The employee who developed a training campaign became an associate director.

Their success is more meaningful to me than any personal accomplishment because it represents the multiplication effect of servant leadership. When you empower one person, you don't just improve one situation; you develop a leader who will go on to empower others, creating ripples that extend far beyond your direct influence.

Practical Next Steps: Decentralization Action Plan

Based on what I've discussed, here's a concrete action plan for implementing decentralized leadership in your organization:

- **Week 1. Assessment and intent**:
    - Assess current decision-making patterns.
    - What decisions are you making that others could make?
    - Write a clear statement of your organization's mission and strategic intent.
    - Identify two to three decisions you can immediately delegate with clear boundaries.
    - Schedule conversations with key team members about empowerment and expectations.

- **Weeks 2–4. Clarity and communication**:
    - Document decision-making authorities at different levels.
    - Communicate this framework clearly to the entire team.
    - Identify training needs that currently prevent effective delegation.

- Begin publicly supporting and celebrating examples of good initiative.

- **Month 2. Infrastructure building**:

    - Establish information-sharing systems so people have context for decisions.
    - Create feedback mechanisms for continuous learning.
    - Set up regular coaching conversations focused on judgment development.
    - Review and remove organizational barriers to decentralized decision-making.

- **Month 3. Expansion and reinforcement**:

    - Expand decision-making authority as people demonstrate capability.
    - Share stories of effective decentralized decisions.
    - Conduct after-action reviews to extract lessons.
    - Assess outcomes. Are decisions happening faster? With better quality? Are people more engaged?

- **Ongoing**:

    - Resist the temptation to recentralize when things get uncomfortable.
    - Continue developing people's decision-making capabilities.
    - Adjust boundaries based on demonstrated competence.
    - Model trust and support even when decisions differ from what you would have chosen.

The goal isn't immediate, perfect decentralization. It's steady progress toward an organization where leadership happens at every level, where people feel genuinely empowered to contribute their best thinking, and where your role evolves from primary decision-maker to enabler of others' success.

Chapter 4

Discipline and Standards: The Framework of Excellence

During my time with the 82nd Airborne, I witnessed something that seemed contradictory to outsiders. The most disciplined units were also the most creative and adaptive. Soldiers who maintained the highest standards were the ones who could think most independently when situations required it. The units with the strictest accountability produced the most confident, self-directed leaders.

This wasn't a paradox at all. It was a fundamental truth about human performance; discipline doesn't constrain excellence, it enables it.

Standards and discipline provide the framework within which true leadership flourishes. They create predictability that allows trust to develop. They establish the baseline that makes exceptional performance recognizable. They build the habits that free the mind to focus on what matters most.

Both military leadership doctrine and servant leadership recognize this truth, though they approach it from different angles. Military leadership emphasizes that standards must be clear, consistent, and universally applied. Servant leadership highlights that standards should be established to serve the mission and the people, not the leader's ego. Together, these philosophies create a powerful approach to building organizational excellence.

Why Standards Matter

Standards are not arbitrary rules imposed to demonstrate authority. They are the codification of what excellence looks like in your organization. They answer the fundamental questions:

- What does good look like?
- What is acceptable?
- What is not?

Without clear standards, every action becomes subjective. People waste energy trying to figure out expectations rather than meeting them. Teams fragment as different members hold different definitions of quality. Leaders exhaust themselves making the same decisions repeatedly because there's no established guideline.

THE COMPONENTS OF EFFECTIVE STANDARDS

Effective standards share several characteristics, whether in a military unit or a civilian organization.

- **Clarity is paramount**: A standard that requires interpretation isn't really a standard; it's a suggestion. "Do your best" isn't a standard. "Complete work accurately" isn't a standard. "All trouble tickets will be acknowledged within two hours and resolved or escalated within 24 hours" is a standard. It's specific, measurable, and leaves no room for confusion.

- **Standards must be achievable but meaningful**: Set them too low, and they become meaningless. Set them too high, and they become demoralizing. The right standard stretches people slightly beyond their comfort zone while remaining within reach of consistent achievement.

I saw this balance play out in the military. Army standards for training are high. They have to be, because we're preparing soldiers for potentially life-or-death situations. But they're also calibrated carefully. The physical fitness standards, weapons qualification requirements, and skills tests are designed to be challenging but achievable for properly trained individuals.

Some new commanders made the mistake of adding their own "higher" standards on top of the Army's requirements, thinking this would produce better soldiers. It rarely worked. Instead, it often created a sense of futility. When soldiers felt that no amount of effort would be sufficient, many stopped trying as hard. The extra standards didn't produce excellence; they produced exhaustion and resentment.

The most effective approach was to maintain the official standards rigorously while providing the training, resources, and support that enabled soldiers to exceed them. Focus on helping people reach the standard, and many will surpass it. Focus on creating unreachable standards, and many won't even achieve the baseline.

- **Standards must be consistently applied**: This is perhaps the most challenging aspect of maintaining standards, and where many leaders fail. It's easy to enforce standards when it's convenient, when you're in a good mood, or when it involves people you don't particularly like.

> It's much harder to enforce them consistently across all situations and all people.

But inconsistent enforcement destroys the credibility of standards faster than anything else. When people see that standards apply only sometimes, or only to some people, they stop taking them seriously. Worse, they lose respect for the leader who selectively enforces them.

STANDARDS AS SERVICE

Here's where servant leadership principles become most important. Standards should serve the mission and the people, not the ego of the leader.

I've seen leaders who established standards simply to demonstrate their authority. Arbitrary rules that existed only to show who was in charge. Procedures that made work harder without making it better. Requirements that checked boxes without adding value.

These aren't real standards; they're power plays. And people see right through them.

Effective standards exist for clear reasons. They ensure quality, enable coordination, protect people, increase efficiency, and support the mission. When you can't articulate why a standard exists beyond "because I said so," it probably shouldn't exist.

This means regularly evaluating standards. Do they still serve their purpose? Has the situation changed in ways that make them obsolete or counterproductive? Are there better ways to achieve the same goal?

Over time, leaders should examine operational standards and ask:

- Is this still necessary?
- Is this still the best way to achieve the goal?
- Have we learned anything that suggests a better approach?

Sometimes my teams have tightened standards because we'd learned they were too loose. Sometimes we relaxed them because we'd learned they were unnecessarily restrictive. Sometimes we changed them entirely because we'd discovered better methods. The key was that standards served us; we didn't serve the standards.

This approach requires humility.

- It means admitting when a standard you established isn't working.
- It means listening when people explain that a requirement is counterproductive.
- It means being willing to change even when change is uncomfortable.

But it also builds tremendous credibility. When your team sees that standards exist to serve genuine purposes, not to serve your ego, they're much more likely to embrace them. When they know you're willing to adjust standards that aren't working, they're more likely to bring problems to your attention rather than working around them.

Standards should be stable enough to provide predictability but flexible enough to adapt to changing circumstances. The key is distinguishing between core principles that don't change and specific applications that should evolve.

During the COVID-19 pandemic, I watched many organizations struggle with this balance. Some clung to pre-pandemic standards that no longer made sense, insisting on procedures designed for in-person work even when everyone was remote. Others abandoned standards entirely, telling people to "just do your best" without clear expectations.

The most effective organizations, including the school district I worked in, maintained core standards while adapting their application:

- Our standard for response time to critical issues didn't change, but we adjusted how we defined and tracked it in a remote environment.
- Our expectation for quality work remained, but we adapted our collaboration methods.
- Our commitment to serving students and teachers intensified, but we changed how that service was delivered.

This required constant communication. We explained what was changing and why, what was staying the same and why, and how people could meet standards in the new context. We asked for feedback about what was working and what wasn't. We adjusted quickly when we got things wrong.

The discipline was in maintaining our commitment to excellence even as the specific expressions of that excellence evolved.

THE ROLE OF DISCIPLINE IN CRISIS

The true test of discipline comes during a crisis. When pressure is high, time is short, and emotions are intense, that's when you discover whether discipline is real or just convenient.

The military faces numerous situations where maintaining discipline is difficult but essential:

- When receiving incoming fire, the discipline of weapons safety prevents friendly casualties.
- When intelligence suggested imminent threats, the discipline of verification prevents tragic mistakes.
- When exhaustion set in after weeks of high operational tempo, the discipline of maintenance keeeps equipment functioning.

In every case, it would be easier in the moment to abandon the discipline. To take shortcuts, to skip steps, to just react. But discipline maintained during a crisis is what separates effective units from dangerous ones.

The same principle applies in civilian crises. When systems fail, when deadlines loom, when stakeholders are demanding immediate results, that's when the temptation to abandon your standards is greatest. And that's exactly when maintaining them matters most.

I've experienced major technology failures. A critical system went down during peak usage, affecting thousands of users. The pressure to "just get it working" was immense. Every minute of downtime generated more complaints, more frustrated users, and more demanding phone calls.

The undisciplined response would have been to start trying random fixes, to skip the standard troubleshooting process, to implement quick patches without proper testing. This might have restored service slightly faster, or it might have made things worse and created additional problems.

Instead, we maintained our disciplined approach:

- We followed our incident response procedures.
- We documented what we tried.
- We tested fixes before implementing them.
- We communicated regularly with stakeholders about what we were doing and why.

The system was restored quickly, probably not much longer than a chaotic approach would have taken, and without creating additional problems or losing the data we needed for root cause analysis. And because we maintained discipline during the crisis, we were able to prevent similar failures in the future.

Discipline during a crisis doesn't mean slowness or bureaucracy. It means following sound procedures even under pressure. It means maintaining the standards that exist precisely because they prevent bad situations from becoming worse.

TEACHING DISCIPLINE WITHOUT BREAKING SPIRIT

One of the most important balancing acts in leadership is developing discipline without crushing initiative, creativity, or morale. This is where servant leadership principles become essential.

Military basic training is sometimes criticized for being too harsh, for "breaking people down." But the best training environments don't break people. They build them up while instilling discipline. There's a crucial difference.

In Basic Training, we had clear standards that were enforced rigorously. Physical fitness requirements, uniform standards, weapons handling procedures, and teamwork expectations—all were nonnegotiable. Soldiers who failed to meet standards faced consequences.

But the environment wasn't designed to crush spirit; it was designed to build confidence through proven competence. The discipline instilled gives soldiers the capability to handle genuinely dangerous situations. The standards maintained kept them safe while they learned. The rigor demanded prepares them for challenges they would face in their military careers.

The key was that discipline was always in service of making soldiers better, not making leaders feel powerful.

- Every standard had a clear purpose.
- Every correction was aimed at improvement.
- Every consequence was designed to develop better performance.

The same approach works in civilian leadership. High standards can be maintained while also supporting people's growth. Discipline also encourages creativity. The key is ensuring that standards serve people's development and the organization's mission, not leadership's egos. This means:

- **Explaining the "why" behind standards**: People are more likely to embrace discipline when they understand its purpose. Take the time to explain why standards exist, what they protect, and what they enable.
- **Providing support along with expectations**: Don't just tell people what the standard is; help them develop the capability to meet it. Training, mentoring, resources, and feedback are all part of building discipline.
- **Recognizing and celebrating progress**: Acknowledge when people improve, even if they haven't yet reached the full standard. Celebrate those who consistently maintain discipline, especially when it's difficult.
- **Maintaining respect even when enforcing standards**: You can address shortfalls without demeaning people. Correction doesn't require humiliation. Accountability doesn't require cruelty.
- **Creating room for growth within the framework**: Standards define the boundaries, but within those, encourage initiative and creativity. Discipline in the fundamentals enables freedom in the details.

Discipline: The Daily Practice of Standards

Standards define excellence. Discipline is the daily practice of pursuing it.

Discipline is often misunderstood, especially in civilian contexts. Many people hear "discipline" and think of punishment, rigidity, or mindless obedience. That's not what discipline means in effective leadership contexts.

True discipline is the consistent application of effort toward a goal, even when motivation wanes. It's the ability to do what needs to be done, when it needs to be done, whether you feel like it or not. It's the bridge between goals and accomplishment.

In the military, it was understood that discipline was fundamentally about self-control and consistency. The disciplined soldier wasn't the one who never made mistakes; they were the ones who maintained standards even when tired, stressed, or afraid. The disciplined unit wasn't the one that performed well only when being watched; it was the one that performed well because that's who they were.

This concept translates directly to civilian leadership. A disciplined team doesn't need constant supervision to do quality work. A disciplined organization doesn't abandon its values when facing pressure. Disciplined individuals don't let temporary feelings override their commitment to excellence.

BUILDING DISCIPLINE IN A TEAM

Leaders don't just practice discipline themselves; they build it in their teams. This is another area where servant leadership principles become especially important. You're not imposing discipline on people; you're helping them develop it for their own benefit and the benefit of the mission.

- **Start with clarity**: People can't be corrected for not meeting vague expectations. Before expecting disciplined performance, what performance looks like must be clearly defined.

  - What are the nonnegotiables?
  - What are the daily standards?
  - What does consistency mean in your context?

- **Define pathways to success**: When I took over a leadership position, one of the first things I would do was work with my team to define our operational disciplines. This created buy-in rather than compliance:

  - What were the daily, weekly, and monthly activities that would ensure we stayed ahead of problems rather than constantly reacting?
  - What were the documentation standards that would ensure knowledge was being shared?
  - What were the communication rhythms that would keep everyone aligned?

- **Model it consistently**: This isn't about perfection; it's about consistency. When you fail to meet your own standards, acknowledge it, correct it, and continue. Your team is watching to see if your disciplines are real or just for show:

  - If you want people to be punctual, be punctual.
  - If you want thorough documentation, document thoroughly.
  - If you want professional communication, communicate professionally.

- **Make it sustainable**: Discipline isn't about temporary intensity; it's about sustainable consistency. This means building discipline that people can maintain long-term via reasonable expectations, adequate resources, and appropriate workloads:

    - A team that works eighty-hour weeks for a month isn't disciplined; they're sprinting—and sprints end.
    - A team that consistently delivers quality work during normal hours, week after week, month after month—that's discipline.
    - You can ask for intensity during genuine crises, but you can't build a culture of sustainable discipline while in constant crisis mode.

- **Provide accountability, with support**: When people fall short of standards, address it. But address it as a leader, not a punisher. The goal is to help people meet the standard, not to make them feel bad about missing it. This might mean:

    - Additional training.
    - Clearer explanations of why the standard matters.
    - Temporary adjustment of workloads to make the standard achievable.
    - In some cases, consequences for repeated failures, but always with the mindset of helping the person succeed.

THE DISCIPLINE OF DEVELOPMENT

One of the most important standards to establish is the expectation of continuous improvement, for yourself and your team.

In the military, we called this "train as you fight." The discipline wasn't just about maintaining current capabilities; it was about constantly developing new ones. Units didn't just practice what they already knew; they pushed beyond their current limits.

This same principle applies in civilian leadership. The discipline of development means consistently investing in capability growth, even when current demands are pressing. It means making time for learning, practicing new skills, and expanding capacity.

When I was working as a network technician and earning my bachelor's, I experienced firsthand how challenging such discipline can be. Working full-time, going to school at night, maintaining family responsibilities—there were countless legitimate reasons to skip the development work.

But I maintained the discipline because I understood that my current role wasn't the final destination. If I wanted to move into leadership, I needed to develop capabilities I didn't currently have. The discipline of development, maintained consistently over years, created opportunities that wouldn't have existed otherwise.

As a leader, I tried to create this same discipline in my teams. Not by mandating development, but by expecting it, supporting it, and modeling it:

- We built professional development time into schedules.
- We created opportunities for people to learn new technologies and take on new responsibilities.
- We celebrated growth and recognized people who expanded their capabilities.

We also established the expectation that standing still wasn't acceptable. Not because we were harsh or demanding, but because we understood that both individuals and organizations that stop developing eventually fall behind. The discipline of continuous improvement became part of who we were.

THE FREEDOM THAT DISCIPLINE CREATES

There is a truth that seems counterintuitive but proves itself repeatedly: discipline creates freedom.

When you and your team maintain consistent standards, you're freed from constant decision-making about basic expectations. When people are disciplined in their core responsibilities, they earn the trust that allows autonomy in other areas. When systems are disciplined, resources are freed for innovation rather than consumed by chaos.

The most creative, adaptive, innovative teams I've led, or been part of, were also the most disciplined. Not despite their discipline, but because of it. The framework of excellence that discipline provides is the foundation on which extraordinary achievement is built.

Standards aren't walls that constrain you; they're the floor that supports you.

The Spectrum of Discipline: From Individual to Organizational

Discipline operates at multiple levels within an organization, and effective leaders must understand and develop it at each level.

INDIVIDUAL DISCIPLINE

This is the foundation. This is the self-control and consistency that each person brings to their work. It's showing up on time, completing commitments, maintaining quality standards, and continuing to perform even when supervision is absent.

During my time in the Army, individual discipline was literally a matter of life and death. When you're operating in a combat zone, you can't have people who only follow safety protocols when someone is watching. You can't have team members who maintain weapons discipline only when it's convenient. Individual discipline had to be so deeply ingrained that it was automatic.

But individual discipline matters just as much in civilian contexts, even if the consequences are less immediately severe.

- The technician who doesn't document their work creates problems that might not surface for months.
- The manager who doesn't follow through on commitments gradually destroys trust.
- The employee who cuts corners when no one is watching creates quality issues that eventually damage the organization.

As a leader, you build individual discipline through clear expectations, consistent accountability, and an environment where disciplined behavior is the norm rather than the exception. When everyone around you maintains standards, you're pulled toward maintaining them yourself. When sloppiness is tolerated, it spreads.

TEAM DISCIPLINE

This emerges when a group of individuals develops shared standards and mutual accountability. The group will begin to function as more than just a collection of individuals, becoming a unit with a collective commitment to excellence.

I saw this most clearly in Basic Training. At the beginning of each cycle, we had a group of individuals with varying levels of personal discipline. Some were highly disciplined; others had never been held to serious standards in their lives. Our job wasn't just to develop individual discipline; it was to forge team discipline.

This happened through several mechanisms. First, we created situations where the team succeeded or failed together. Physical training in formation, team competitions, group problem-solving exercises—activities where individual performance affected collective outcomes. This built peer accountability naturally.

Second, we established team standards that went beyond individual performance. How soldiers treated each other, how they communicated, and how they supported struggling team members became part of the team's identity. Soldiers who maintained high personal standards but undermined team cohesion were corrected, because team discipline requires both individual excellence and collective commitment.

Third, we gave teams increasing autonomy as they demonstrated discipline. Early in the cycle, everything was tightly supervised. As the team showed they could maintain standards without constant oversight, we stepped back. This created a cycle. Discipline earned trust, trust enabled autonomy, and autonomy reinforced discipline because the team didn't want to lose it.

In civilian contexts, team discipline looks different but matters just as much. A technology support team that maintains consistent response times, thorough documentation, and professional service—even during peak periods or when leadership is absent—demonstrates team discipline. A management team that maintains productive meeting practices, follows through on commitments, and holds each other accountable shows team discipline.

ORGANIZATIONAL DISCIPLINE

The most complex level. This is embedding discipline in the culture, systems, and processes of the entire organization. It's no longer dependent on specific individuals or teams; it's become part of how the organization operates.

Building organizational discipline has always been one of my primary goals as a leader. With people across multiple locations and responsibilities, I couldn't personally supervise everyone. Team leaders could only oversee their immediate teams. We needed discipline to be woven into the organizational fabric.

We did this through several approaches:

- **Standard operating procedures**: Documented how we handled common situations. Not bureaucratic manuals that nobody read, but practical guides that made disciplined approaches easier than undisciplined ones. When someone wasn't sure how to handle a situation, they had a resource that codified our standards.
- **Systems and tools**: Built discipline into workflows. Our ticketing system automatically escalated issues that weren't acknowledged within specified timeframes. Our project management tools made status reporting a natural part of progress tracking. Our documentation system made knowledge sharing an integrated part of problem resolution. These systems didn't replace discipline; they supported it.
- **Hiring and onboarding practices**: Selected for and developed discipline. We looked for people who demonstrated consistent performance in previous roles. During onboarding, we explicitly taught our standards and why they mattered. New employees learned quickly that discipline wasn't just expected from some people; it was how everyone operated.
- **Recognition and advancement systems**: Rewarded disciplined performance. People who consistently maintained standards, even when it was difficult, were the ones who advanced. The message was clear. We value discipline here, not just results achieved through any means.
- **Leadership consistency across all levels**: My leadership team and I modeled discipline relentlessly. We main-

tained the same standards we expected from others. When we made mistakes, we acknowledged them and corrected them. Over time, this consistency created an organizational culture where discipline was simply "how we do things."

Building organizational discipline takes years, not months. It requires persistent leadership, consistent messaging, and patience as the culture shifts. But once established, it becomes self-reinforcing. New people are pulled into the culture of discipline. Lapses are corrected by peers, not just by management. Standards are maintained because that's the organizational identity, not because someone is enforcing them.

Common Pitfalls in Establishing Standards and Discipline

Even well-intentioned leaders make predictable mistakes when establishing standards and building discipline. Avoiding these pitfalls will accelerate progress:

- **Too many standards**: When everything is important, nothing is important. Leaders who try to establish standards for every aspect of work create cognitive overload. People can't remember fifty different standards, so they end up following none of them consistently. Focus on the vital few. What are the three to five standards that truly matter for the mission and your people? Establish these clearly and maintain them rigorously. Once they're embedded in the culture, you can add others. But start with ruthless prioritization.

- **Standards without resources**: Expecting people to meet standards without providing adequate time, training, tools, or support is a recipe for frustration. It's the equivalent of assigning a combat mission without providing ammunition. Before establishing a standard, ensure people have what they need to meet it. If rapid response times are expected, ensure adequate staffing. If thorough documentation is demanded, provide the tools and training to do so efficiently. If professional communication is prioritized, teach communication skills to those who lack them.
- **Punishment-focused enforcement**: Leaders who only address standards when they're violated, and only through negative consequences, create a culture of fear rather than excellence. People focus on avoiding punishment rather than pursuing excellence. Effective enforcement includes recognition of those who meet standards, support for those who struggle, and consequences only when other approaches have failed. The goal is to help people succeed, not to catch them failing.
- **Leader exemption**: The fastest way to destroy standards is for leaders to exempt themselves from them. When you establish a standard for punctuality but regularly show up late to meetings, you've communicated that the standard isn't real. When expecting thorough documentation from the team, but don't document your decisions, your credibility is undermined. Leaders must hold themselves to the same standards—actually, to higher standards—than they expect from their teams. Your behavior sets the real standard, not your words.
- **Rigidity in application**: Standards provide the framework, but judgment is still required in their application. Leaders who apply standards without considering context, using

discretion, or adapting to exceptional circumstances create resentment. The goal is consistent application, not mindless application. When someone misses a deadline because of a genuine emergency, that's different from someone missing it due to poor planning. When circumstances genuinely warrant an exception, make it—but make it consciously and explain your reasoning.
- **Standards that serve the leader, not the mission**: I once worked with a leader who required weekly written reports from every team member, formatted in a very specific way, delivered at exactly 5:00 PM every Friday. When asked why, he couldn't articulate how these reports served the mission. They were simply how he wanted to receive information. These reports consumed significant time, provided little value, and were resented by the team.

Don't create standards just because you like them or because they make you feel in control. Every standard should serve a clear purpose, not just personal preference.

Building A Framework

While establishing discipline and standards in an organization, consider these practices:

- **Define nonnegotiables**: What are the three to five standards that are absolutely essential to your mission? What must be maintained regardless of circumstances? Be selective; everything can't be nonnegotiable.
- **Make standards visible**: Document them clearly. Display them prominently. Reference them regularly. Standards

that exist only in your head or buried in forgotten documents aren't real standards.

- **Connect standards to purpose**: Help people understand why each standard exists. What does it protect? What does it enable? How does it serve the mission and the people? Standards with clear purpose are embraced; standards without purpose are resented.
- **Create systems that support discipline**: Don't just expect people to remember and follow standards through sheer willpower. Build them into workflows, checklists, templates, and processes. Make the disciplined path the easy path.
- **Celebrate adherence, not just results**: Recognize people who consistently maintain standards, especially when it's difficult. This reinforces that the process matters, not just the outcome.
- **Address violations quickly and privately**: When someone falls short of standards, address it promptly. But do it privately, with respect, and with the goal of understanding and improving rather than punishing.
- **Review and refine regularly**: Set a recurring time to evaluate standards. Are they still relevant? Are they working as intended? What have you learned that should inform changes?
- **Lead by example relentlessly**: Your discipline will do more to establish standards than any policy or procedure. Show what consistency looks like, especially when it's hard.

Put It into Practice

To establish standards and build discipline in an organization, start with these actions:

- **This week:**
    - Identify the three most critical standards for the team or organization.
    - Document them clearly. What they are, why they matter, and what meeting them looks like.
    - Honestly assess your adherence to these standards.
- **This month:**
    - Communicate these standards to the team with clear explanations of their purpose.
    - Identify what resources, training, or support people need to meet the standards.
    - Establish a system for recognizing those who consistently maintain standards.
    - Begin addressing violations promptly and constructively.
- **This quarter:**
    - Review whether standards are being maintained consistently.
    - Assess whether they're serving their intended purpose.
    - Identify one additional standard to introduce (if needed) or one existing standard to refine.
    - Evaluate your discipline track record. Where are you modeling excellence, and where do you need to improve?

Remember, discipline isn't the enemy of creativity, initiative, or morale. Done correctly, it's the foundation that enables all three. Standards don't constrain excellence; they define it and make it achievable.

Chapter 5

Communication: The Leader's Essential Tool

In the summer of 2006, I sat in an operations center in Iraq, watching a critical mission unfold on multiple screens. Reports were streaming in, units were maneuvering, and decisions needed to be made quickly. But what struck me most that night wasn't the technology or the tactics. It was the clarity and precision of the communication.

Soldiers spoke in calm, measured tones. They acknowledged every transmission and confirmed understanding. They asked clarifying questions when needed. They never assumed. And when plans changed, as they always do in combat, changes were communicated clearly, verified for understanding, and ensured everyone knew their role.

That night, every soldier came home safely. The mission succeeded. And a primary reason was communication: clear, disciplined, intentional communication.

Communication is the leader's essential tool. It's how you cast vision, build trust, provide direction, offer feedback, resolve conflict, and create culture. Without effective communication, every other leadership skill becomes nearly useless. You can have the best strategy, the highest standards, and the most servant-hearted intentions, but if you can't communicate them effectively, you can't lead effectively.

The military has always understood this. That's why radio discipline is drilled relentlessly, clear and concise briefings are mandatory, and every operation includes a detailed communication plan. The military emphasized practical, no-nonsense communication that got the job done without unnecessary complexity.

Servant leadership adds a crucial dimension to military communication practices: empathy. The best leaders don't just communicate clearly; they communicate in ways that connect with their audience. They listen as much as they speak. They adapt their message to their audience. They create space for dialogue, not just monologue.

This chapter explores the critical role communication plays in leadership. I'll examine the principles of clear military communication, the empathetic practices of servant leadership communication, and how to integrate both in daily leadership.

The Military Communication Standard

Military communication follows a simple but powerful principle, which is that clarity saves lives. In combat, miscommunication can mean the difference between mission success and catastrophic failure. That's why the military has developed rigorous communication standards that have been refined over decades of experience.

The Five Cs of military communication:

1. **Clear**: Use simple language, avoid jargon (unless speaking to those who share that vocabulary), which will eliminate ambiguity.

2. **Concise**: Say what needs to be said—nothing more, nothing less.
3. **Complete**: Include all necessary information; don't make people guess or assume.
4. **Confirmed**: Verify that your message was received and understood as intended.
5. **Controlled**: Discipline your communication; think before you speak.

During my time with the 82nd Airborne, I witnessed these principles in action daily. Before every jump, the jumpmaster would brief the entire chalk (military jargon for soldiers deployed from aircraft). The brief followed a standard format. Every critical point was stated clearly. Questions were allowed. Understanding was verified. Nothing was left to chance.

This wasn't bureaucracy for its own sake; it was recognition that when paratroopers exit an aircraft at 1,250 feet traveling 130 knots, there's no room for confusion. Everyone must know the plan, their role, the contingencies, and how to communicate in the air and on the ground.

The same principle was applied in the psychological operations world. When we crafted messages intended to influence enemy forces or reassure local populations, every word mattered. Ambiguity could undermine the entire operation. Cultural misunderstanding could turn potential allies into adversaries. We drafted, reviewed, tested, and refined our communication until it conveyed exactly what we intended—no more, no less.

THE BATTLE ROSTER CHECK

One of the most powerful communication practices I learned in the military was the battle roster check. After every significant event—a movement, an attack, a patrol—leaders would account for every person in their unit. They would verify that everyone was present, everyone was okay, and everyone understood what happened and what comes next.

This practice did more than confirm head counts. It created a rhythm of regular, structured communication. It ensured that leaders stayed connected to their people. It provided opportunities to identify problems early. And it demonstrated that every person mattered enough to be counted and checked on.

I adapted this practice in my civilian leadership. I would connect with each of my direct reports every week, even if just for five minutes. Not to micromanage, but to check in. To make sure they were okay. To see if they needed anything. To keep communication lines open.

This simple practice prevented countless small problems from becoming big ones. It kept me connected to what was actually happening in my organization. And it sent a clear message: you matter, your work matters, and I'm paying attention.

The Servant Leadership Communication Approach

While military communication emphasizes clarity and efficiency, servant leadership adds the dimension of empathy and connection. Servant leaders recognize that communication isn't just about transmitting information, but about building relationships, understanding perspectives, and creating shared meaning.

ACTIVE LISTENING

The foundation of servant leadership communication is active listening. This goes far beyond just hearing words; it means fully engaging with what someone is saying, understanding their perspective, acknowledging their feelings, and responding thoughtfully.

Active listening requires:

- **Full attention**: Put down the phone, close your laptop, make eye contact, be present.
- **Suspending judgment**: Listen to understand, not to prepare a rebuttal.
- **Asking clarifying questions**: Ensure you truly understand what's being communicated.
- **Reflecting back**: Paraphrase what you heard to confirm understanding.
- **Acknowledging emotions**: Recognize and validate feelings, not just facts.

During my time as CIO, one of my technicians came to my office visibly frustrated. She launched into a complaint about a new organizational structure I had implemented. My initial instinct was to defend my decision and explain why the procedure was necessary. I wanted to show maps with colored lines.

Instead, I stopped, listened, asked questions, and reflected on what I was hearing. And as I listened, I realized she wasn't actually opposed to the structure itself. She was frustrated because she hadn't been consulted before it was implemented, and in fairness, the procedure didn't account for several realities she dealt with in the field.

By listening actively, I discovered that my decision wasn't wrong, but my decision-making and communication process had been incomplete. I had announced a change without explaining the reasoning, without seeking input, and without considering implementation challenges.

We revised the structure. It became better because of her input. And our relationship grew stronger because she felt heard and valued.

ADAPTING YOUR MESSAGE

Effective communicators adapt their message to their audience. The same information needs to be communicated differently to different groups.

When I briefed senior military commanders, I led with the bottom line, provided essential context, and stood ready to answer detailed questions. They needed actionable information quickly.

When I briefed my team, I provided more context about the strategic situation, explained how our mission fit into the bigger picture, and sought their input on execution. They needed to understand the "why" to be effective.

When we communicated with the local population in Iraq through our products, we used simple language, culturally appropriate imagery, and messages that resonated with their values and concerns. They needed information that made sense in their context.

The same principle applies in civilian leadership. When I communicated technology initiatives to the school board, I focused on outcomes and return on investment. When I communicated with teachers, I emphasized how technology would help them serve students better. When I communicated with my technical team, I provided the technical details and implementation challenges.

Same initiative. Different audiences, different communication approaches. All effective because they were tailored to the audience's needs, knowledge level, and concerns.

VULNERABILITY AND AUTHENTICITY

Servant leaders communicate with appropriate vulnerability and authenticity. They don't pretend to have all the answers. They admit mistakes, share struggles, and show their humanity.

This doesn't mean oversharing or burdening a team with your personal problems. It means being real, honest, and creating a culture where people can do the same.

After being laid off from my software company, I struggled with confidence. When I eventually found my calling in education technology, I could have hidden that struggle. Instead, when the opportunity arose, I shared it.

I told others about being laid off. About the self-doubt and wondering if I'd find meaningful work again. And about how that struggle taught me resilience, humility, and gratitude for the opportunity to serve.

That authenticity created connection. Team members who were facing their own struggles felt comfortable talking with me about theirs. People who had experienced job loss or career uncertainty knew I understood. And everyone saw that failure isn't fatal, that it's often the path to growth.

Integrating Military Precision with Servant Leadership Empathy

The most effective leadership communication integrates military precision with servant leadership empathy. You communicate clearly, concisely, and completely, while also listening actively, adapting to your audience, and connecting authentically.

THE COMMUNICATION PLANNING PROCESS

Before any significant communication, effective leaders plan their approach:

- **Define the purpose**: What do you need to accomplish with this communication?
- **Know your audience**: Who are you communicating with? What do they need? What do they already know?
- **Craft your message**: What's the core message? What supporting information is needed?
- **Choose your method**: Face-to-face? Email? Meeting? Memo? What's most effective for this message and audience?
- **Anticipate questions**: What will people want to know? What concerns might they have?
- **Plan for feedback**: How will you verify understanding? How will you gather input?
- **Follow up**: How will you reinforce the message and address ongoing questions?

This might seem like a lot of work for everyday communication, but it becomes second nature with practice. And for critical communications—announcing major changes, addressing crises, providing difficult feedback—this process is essential.

THE CHANGE COMMUNICATION EXAMPLE

When I needed to reorganize my technology department to better align with district needs, I knew the communication would be critical. The reorganization affected everyone. Some people would gain responsibility, while others would shift to different teams. Everyone would wonder how it affected them.

Here's how I applied the communication planning process:

- **Purpose**: Explain the reorganization, help people understand the reasoning, address concerns, and maintain morale and trust through the transition.
- **Audience**: My entire department, which included technical staff at various levels with varying lengths of service, different work styles, and different concerns.
- **Core message**: We're reorganizing to better serve our schools and students. This change will improve our effectiveness and create better opportunities for growth. Everyone's role remains valued and important.
- **Method**: Multiple. First, a department-wide meeting to announce and explain; second, individual meetings with each affected person; third, written documentation that everyone could reference; fourth, regular check-ins during the transition.
- **Anticipated questions**: Why now? How does this affect me? What if I don't want to change teams? Who will I report to? What about my current projects?
- **Feedback plan**: Questions during the announcement meeting, individual conversations, an anonymous survey two weeks later, and an open-door policy for ongoing concerns.
- **Follow-up**: Weekly department updates during the transition, monthly reviews after implementation, and a six-month assessment.

The reorganization wasn't easy. Change never is. But the communication approach made it manageable. People understood the reasons. They had opportunities to voice concerns. They knew what to expect. And because the communication was clear, empathetic, and consistent, trust remained strong.

Difficult Conversations: When Communication Matters Most

Leadership communication is most critical, and most challenging, during difficult conversations. Providing corrective feedback, addressing performance problems, delivering bad news, and navigating conflict—these situations test your communication skills and your character.

THE FEEDBACK CONVERSATION

Providing corrective feedback is one of leadership's most critical communication responsibilities. Done well, it builds trust, improves performance, and strengthens relationships. Done poorly, it damages morale, creates defensiveness, and erodes confidence.

Effective feedback conversations require careful preparation and disciplined execution. They are not casual exchanges or off-the-cuff corrections. They demand your full attention and best communication skills.

The framework for effective feedback:

- **Privacy and timing**: Schedule private feedback conversations; never have them in front of others. Public correction humiliates rather than educates. Choose a time when both you and the team member can focus without distraction or time pressure. Rushed feedback conversations rarely achieve their purpose.
- **Specific observation**: Describe the specific behavior or performance issue that has been observed. Use concrete facts, not general impressions. "You've been late to the morning briefing four times in the past two weeks" is actionable. "You seem uncommitted lately" is not. Avoid

character judgments. Focus on observable actions and measurable results. The goal is to address behavior that can be changed, not to attack someone's identity or worth.

- **Clear impact**: Explain the consequences of the behavior. How does it affect the mission, the team, the organization, or the individual's development? People are more likely to change when they understand why the change matters. Connect the specific behavior to larger principles or goals. Help the person see how their actions align, or don't, with the standards and values that have been established collectively.
- **Genuine inquiry**: Ask questions before drawing conclusions. "Help me understand what's going on?" or "What's your perspective on this?" demonstrates respect and invites dialogue. This isn't a formality. Listen actively to the response. Sometimes the observed behavior stems from obstacles you didn't know existed, misunderstandings you didn't anticipate, or circumstances you didn't consider. Your role is to understand the full situation before prescribing solutions.
- **Collaborative problem-solving**: Once you understand the situation completely, work together to identify solutions. In many cases, the team member will have better ideas about how to address the issue than you do. Your job is to ensure accountability, not to micromanage the path forward. Agree on specific next steps, timelines, and measures of success. Vague commitments like "I'll do better" accomplish nothing. Clear agreements like "I'll submit weekly reports by noon every Friday for the next month" create accountability.
- **Follow-up and support**: Feedback isn't complete when the meeting ends. Follow up regularly to track progress,

provide support, and recognize improvement. If the person makes the agreed-upon changes, acknowledge it. If they don't, address it promptly. Effective feedback is a process, not an event. It requires sustained attention and consistent follow-through.

Feedback conversations test communication skills and commitment to your people. They're uncomfortable. They require emotional energy. They're easy to postpone or avoid.

- **Timeliness**: Address issues promptly. Feedback delayed is feedback diminished. Waiting weeks to address a problem signals that either the issue doesn't matter or you're uncomfortable with direct communication. Neither message serves your leadership position.
- **Balance**: Provide positive feedback as consistently as corrective feedback. If the only time you offer detailed feedback is when something goes wrong, people learn to dread conversations with you. Recognize excellence with the same specificity and thoughtfulness you use to address problems.
- **Consistency**: Apply the same standards to everyone. Nothing destroys credibility faster than selective enforcement of expectations. If you address tardiness with one team member, you must address it with all team members.
- **Developmental intent**: Approach feedback as a tool for growth, not punishment. The goal is to help people improve, not to demonstrate authority or superiority. This mindset shapes tone, word choice, and listening skills.

Leaders who master feedback conversations build stronger teams, higher performance, and deeper trust than leaders who shy away from them.

DELIVERING BAD NEWS

Leadership inevitably requires delivering news people don't want to hear:

- Budget cuts.
- Position eliminations.
- Failed initiatives.
- Policy changes that create hardship.
- Mission outcomes that fall short of expectations.

The ability to communicate bad news with clarity, honesty, and compassion directly impacts how your team responds. Handle it well, and people will trust you even in difficult circumstances. Handle it poorly, and you'll lose credibility that may never be fully regained.

- **Ownership**: If you made the decision or participated in making it, own it. Don't hide behind "they decided" or "the organization chose." Use "I" language when appropriate. Leaders who deflect responsibility during difficult conversations lose credibility.
- **Consistency**: Ensure that everyone who needs to hear the news hears it from you in roughly the same timeframe. Nothing creates more dysfunction than people learning about significant changes via informal channels before official communication occurs.

- **Humanity**: Remember that behind every difficult conversation is a person with concerns, obligations, and emotions. Professional communication doesn't mean emotionless communication. It means respectful, clear, honest communication that acknowledges the human impact of difficult decisions.

Delivering bad news is never pleasant. But it's a nonnegotiable leadership responsibility. Willingness to communicate difficult information directly, honestly, and compassionately defines character as a leader. This will determine whether your team will trust you when circumstances are hard.

Utilize the following framework for delivering bad news.

Privacy and Respect

Deliver bad news that affects individuals privately, face-to-face when possible. People deserve to hear difficult information directly from their leader, not through organizational announcements or secondhand reports.

For news that affects the entire team or organization, consider whether individual conversations should precede or follow the group announcement. Sometimes people need private context before a public discussion; sometimes they need time to process privately after hearing news in a group setting.

Never deliver personally significant bad news through email or text message unless physical distance makes face-to-face communication impossible. The medium chosen communicates how much you value the person receiving the news.

Directness Without Delay

Don't bury bad news in preliminary context or softening language. State the essential message clearly at the beginning of the conversation. "I need to tell you that your position is being eliminated" is direct. Spending ten minutes discussing budget challenges before revealing the decision is torture, not kindness.

Directness demonstrates respect. It acknowledges that the person can handle difficult information without elaborate emotional preparation. It also ensures clarity; there's no risk they'll miss the message because you obscured it with a rambling preamble.

Complete Honesty

Explain the situation fully and truthfully. What decision was made? Why? What alternatives were considered? What factors drove the outcome?

Avoid corporate euphemisms, bureaucratic language, or vague explanations that obscure responsibility. "Your position was eliminated due to budget constraints" is honest. "We're going in a different direction," or "It's just the way things worked out," are evasive.

If there are aspects of the situation you can't discuss—personnel matters, confidential deliberations, legal constraints—say so explicitly. "I can't share details about that part of the process because of personnel privacy" is acceptable. Pretending those constraints don't exist and offering incomplete explanations is not.

Acknowledgment of Impact

Recognize that the news is difficult. Don't minimize the disappointment, frustration, or hardship the person or team will experience. Phrases like "I know this is hard" or "I recognize this isn't what you hoped for" validate the emotional response without becoming overly dramatic.

Avoid false optimism or platitudes. "Everything happens for a reason" or "This will turn out to be a blessing" may feel comforting to you, but they often ring hollow to the person receiving bad news. Your job is to acknowledge reality, not to reframe it prematurely.

Actionable Information

Provide every detail you can about what happens next. Outline timelines, processes, and resources available. The next steps available, the questions to ask, and the points of contact moving forward.

Bad news becomes more manageable when people understand what to expect and what they can control. Ambiguity amplifies anxiety. Clarity, even about difficult circumstances, provides a sense of agency.

If you don't have all the information yet, say so. Commit to providing updates as soon as you know more. Then follow through on that commitment.

Space for Response

Give people time to process, ask questions, and express their reactions. Don't rush them toward acceptance or attempt to manage their emotional response. Some people will need to vent frustration. Some will need silence, while some will need detailed questions answered. Your job is to be present and responsive, not to control their reaction or move quickly to closure.

Sustained Support

The conversation doesn't end when the meeting does. Check in regularly. Offer whatever support is within your power to provide. Follow through on commitments made during the initial conversation. If the bad news affects someone's livelihood or professional standing, consider what you can do to help them move forward, like references, introductions, advocacy, and recommendations. Your obligation as a leader extends beyond the immediate moment.

Communication in Crisis

Crisis situations demand the highest level of communication skills. When things go wrong, how you communicate can mean the difference between panic and calm, chaos and coordinated response, and destroyed trust and strengthened confidence.

Here are the crisis communication principles.

- **Communicate early and often**: Don't wait until you have all the answers. Acknowledge the situation quickly, explain what you know, and commit to regular updates. Silence creates anxiety and speculation. When our internet access was lost during payroll processing, I sent the first communication as soon as we were aware of the problem, before even fully understanding it. "We're aware of the system outage. Our team is actively working on it. We'll provide updates every hour." That immediate acknowledgment prevented panic and rumor. People knew we were aware and working on it.
- **Be honest about what you don't know**: Don't speculate or make promises you can't keep. It's okay to say, "I don't know yet, but here's what we're doing to find out." Honesty builds trust; false reassurance destroys it.
- **Focus on what you're doing**: People want to know action is being taken. Explain the steps being taken to address the situation, even if you can't promise immediate resolution. During the system outage, every update included what we had discovered, what we were currently doing,

and what the next step would be. People could see progress, even when the problem wasn't solved yet.

- **Set realistic expectations**: Don't over-promise; always under-promise and over-deliver. If you think it will take six hours to fix, say eight hours and finish in six. Allow for the unexpected to impact your timeline.
- **Acknowledge impact and emotion**: Recognize how the crisis affects people. Don't minimize legitimate concerns or frustrations. "I know this outage is creating significant frustration and extra work. Your concerns are valid and understandable."
- **Provide clear next steps**: Tell people what they should do, what to expect, and how they'll know when the situation is resolved.

THE AFTER-ACTION COMMUNICATION

After any crisis, effective leaders conduct and communicate an after-action review.

- What happened?
- Why?
- What did we do well?
- What could we improve?
- What are we changing to prevent recurrence?

This demonstrates accountability, commitment to improvement, and turns a crisis into a learning opportunity.

After the system outage, I sent an update to all stakeholders. I explained the technical cause, our response, what worked in our response, what we could have done better, and the specific changes we were implementing to prevent future occurrences.

Several people told me that the report increased their confidence in our department more than if the outage had never happened. They saw accountability, honesty, and commitment to improvement.

Building a Communication Culture

Individual communication skills matter, but the most effective leaders build a culture where good communication is the norm, not the exception.

REGULAR COMMUNICATION RHYTHMS

Establish appropriate and predictable communication patterns so people know when and how they'll receive information:

- **Daily huddles**: Quick team check-ins to start the day aligned.
- **Weekly, bi-weekly, or monthly one-on-ones**: Individual time with each direct report.
- **Monthly team meetings**: Broader updates, discussion, and team building.
- **Quarterly all-hands**: Big picture vision, accomplishments, direction.
- **Annual planning sessions**: Strategic thinking and goal setting.

These rhythms create structure, which reduces anxiety and ensures important information flows consistently.

MULTIPLE COMMUNICATION CHANNELS

Different messages need different channels. Effective leaders use the right channel for each message:

- **Face-to-face**: Best for difficult conversations, complex topics, building relationships, brainstorming, or anything requiring discussion.
- **Video calls**: Good for remote team connection, when face-to-face isn't possible, and visual presentations are necessary.
- **Phone calls**: Good for quick questions, urgent matters, and personal check-ins when video isn't needed.
- **Email**: Good for detailed information that people will need to reference, nonurgent updates, documentation, or anything requiring a written record.
- **Instant messaging**: Good for quick questions, coordination, and informal communication, though it can be overused and interrupt focus.
- **Meetings**: Good for collaboration, decision-making, and complex discussion, but should be used sparingly and efficiently.
- **Written memos/announcements**: Good for formal communications, policy changes, and important updates that need documentation.

One thing that can hinder effective communication is email. People often send long, detailed emails about changes or initiatives, then wonder why people seem confused or disconnected.

Email is great for information, but terrible for connection and understanding. Important messages need face-to-face or video communication first, with email as follow-up documentation.

THE COMMUNICATION FEEDBACK LOOP

Build mechanisms to ensure communication is working well:

- **Ask directly**: "Does this make sense?" "What questions do you have?" "What am I missing?"
- **Check understanding**: Have people summarize back what they heard.
- **Observe behavior**: Are people doing what you communicated? If not, the communication probably wasn't effective.
- **Create safe feedback channels**: Anonymous surveys, suggestion boxes, and open-door policies.
- **Act on feedback**: When people tell you communication isn't working, believe them and adjust.

Practical Communication Skills for Daily Leadership

Effective communication isn't just about major announcements and crisis management. It's about the daily interactions that build relationships and get work done.

THE EFFECTIVE BRIEF

Whether presenting to your boss, team, or stakeholders, an effective brief follows a basic structure:

- **Bottom line up front (BLUF)**: Lead with the main point or recommendation.
- **Background**: Provide essential context (briefly).

- **Analysis**: Explain your reasoning or the situation assessment.
- **Recommendation**: What should we do? (if applicable).
- **Discussion**: Open for questions and input.

This structure respects people's time and ensures the most important information comes first.

THE EFFECTIVE EMAIL

Work emails should:

- **Include a subject line that clearly indicates the content**: People should know what the email is about before opening.
- **Have the purpose stated in the first sentence**: Don't bury the lead.
- **Be brief and organized**: Use bullet points, headers, and short paragraphs.
- **Be clear on required action**: What do you need the recipient to do? By when?
- **Be of an appropriate length**: If it takes more than two or three paragraphs to explain, you probably need to communicate in a different way.

THE EFFECTIVE MEETING

Meetings should be:

- **Necessary**: Could this be an email or quick conversation instead?

- **Clearly purposed**: Everyone should know why we're meeting.
- **Properly attended**: Only people who need to be there.
- **Time-bounded**: Start on time, end on time (or early), and never start late.
- **Documented**: Notes capturing decisions, action items, and next steps.
- **Action-oriented**: End with clear next steps and accountability.

My current organization has a clear meeting standard. Employees are trained in the process. There are agenda templates used regularly. It's part of the culture. Our meetings are some of the most productive of any organization I've ever been in.

THE EFFECTIVE ONE-ON-ONE

Individual meetings with team members should:

- **Be regular and protected**: Don't cancel unless absolutely necessary.
- **Recognize that it is their time, not yours**: Let them set the agenda.
- **Be balanced between support and accountability**: "How can I help you?" and "How's progress on your goals?"
- **Include space for honest conversation**: Creates psychological safety.
- **Be forward-looking**: Focus on future success, not just past problems.

My one-on-ones became the most valuable leadership communication tool. They prevented small issues from becoming big ones. They built trust. They kept me connected to what was really happening. And they gave my team members dedicated time with me, regardless of how busy things got.

Communication and Remote/Hybrid Work

The shift to remote and hybrid work has made communication both more important and more challenging. You can't rely on hallway conversations, visual cues, or casual check-ins when the team is distributed.

Remote communication best practices include:

- **Over-communicate**: What might feel like too much communication is probably just right when working remotely. Share updates, context, and information liberally.
- **Use video**: When possible, use video for meetings and one-on-ones. Seeing faces creates a connection that audio alone doesn't provide.
- **Be intentional about informal communication**: Create space for the kind of casual interaction that happens naturally in offices but requires intentionality to happen remotely. Virtual coffee chats, non-work Slack channels, and brief personal check-ins.
- **Document more**: When you can't just walk over to someone's desk, good documentation becomes critical. Write things down, share files, and use collaborative tools.
- **Respect boundaries**: Remote work blurs the line between work and home. Be mindful of not contacting people outside work hours unless truly urgent.
- **Check in on well-being**: Remote workers can feel isolated. Regular check-ins that include "How are you really doing?" matter even more.

Communication Across Cultures and Generations

As a leader, you'll often communicate with people from different backgrounds, cultures, and generations. Effective communication requires awareness of these differences and the flexibility to adapt.

CULTURAL COMMUNICATION CONSIDERATIONS

During my deployment to Iraq, I knew that effective communication with local populations required understanding cultural context. Direct communication styles that worked well with American soldiers could be perceived as rude or aggressive in Iraqi culture. Conversely, the indirect communication common in Iraqi culture could seem evasive to Americans expecting straightforward answers.

I learned to:

- Research cultural norms before communicating across cultures.
- Ask questions and do research about preferred communication styles rather than assuming.
- Pay attention to nonverbal cues, which vary significantly across cultures.
- Use simple, clear language and avoid idioms that don't translate well.
- Verify understanding more carefully when language or cultural barriers exist.
- Show respect for different communication preferences.

These same principles applied in my civilian role leading a diverse technology department. Team members from different cultural backgrounds had different expectations about hierarchy, directness, formality, and feedback.

GENERATIONAL COMMUNICATION DIFFERENCES

My technology department spanned four generations, from Baby Boomers nearing retirement to Gen Z employees just starting their careers. Each generation had different communication preferences and expectations.

- **Baby Boomers (1946–1964) often preferred**:
    - Face-to-face or phone communication for important matters.
    - More formal communication styles.
    - Detailed explanations and context.
    - Respect for hierarchy and established processes.
- **Gen X (1965–1980) often preferred**:
    - Direct, efficient communication.
    - Independence and autonomy.
    - Skepticism of corporate-speak.
    - Work-life balance considerations in communication timing.
- **Millennials (1981–1996) often preferred**:
    - Frequent feedback and communication.
    - Collaborative approaches.
    - Purpose and meaning in work.

  - Multiple communication channels, including digital.
  - Flexibility in when and how they communicate.

- **Gen Z (1997–2012) often preferred**:

  - Digital-first communication.
  - Visual and video content.
  - Authenticity and transparency.
  - Quick, brief interactions.
  - Social responsibility considerations.

These are generalizations, not rules. Individuals vary widely within generations. But being aware of generational tendencies helped me communicate more effectively. I learned to:

- **Use multiple channels**: Reach everyone effectively.
- **Explain the "why"**: Millennials and Gen Z particularly valued this.
- **Provide both autonomy and support**: Balancing Gen X independence with Millennial collaboration needs.
- **Offer options**: Both digital and in-person options when possible.
- **Be flexible**: Adapt formality levels based on the audience.
- **Be authentic**: This resonates across all generations but is especially important to younger employees.

The key wasn't choosing one generation's preferences over another; it was being flexible enough to communicate effectively with everyone.

Storytelling in Leadership Communication

One of the most powerful communication tools leaders have is storytelling. Stories engage emotions, make abstract concepts concrete, help people remember messages, and create connections.

During military briefings and civilian meetings, I noticed that PowerPoint slides full of data would quickly lose the audience. But when a presentation included a story with a real example of the concept being discussed, everyone leaned in and paid attention.

Stories work because:

- **They're memorable**: People forget statistics but remember stories.
- **They're relatable**: Stories help people see themselves in the situation.
- **They're emotional**: Stories engage hearts as well as minds.
- **They're concrete**: Stories make abstract principles tangible.
- **They're persuasive**: Stories bypass logical resistance and connect directly.

USING STORIES EFFECTIVELY

Effective leadership stories should:

- **Be relevant**: They should be related to the point you're making.
- **Be true**: If not, clearly label them as hypothetical.
- **Be appropriate in length**: Short stories illustrate points; long stories lose attention.
- **Include specific details**: This makes them more vivid.

- **Have a clear takeaway**: One that connects to your message.
- **Personal vulnerability**: Some of the most powerful leadership stories involve appropriate vulnerability, like sharing your own failures, struggles, and lessons learned.

When I've talked about being laid off from the software company, struggling with confidence, and finding my calling in education technology and service, I created a connection with team members who had faced similar challenges.

When I shared stories about leadership mistakes I have made, times I had communicated poorly, made wrong decisions, or failed to support someone effectively, I created a culture where admitting mistakes was acceptable and learning from them was expected.

The key is "appropriate" vulnerability. Share enough to create a connection and demonstrate humanity, but not so much that you burden a team with your problems or undermine their confidence in your leadership.

Communication and Organizational Culture

The way leaders communicate shapes organizational culture. Communication patterns—what is talked about, what is ignored, how problems are responded to, what is celebrated, how feedback is delivered—send powerful messages about what's valued and expected. It's culture-building communication.

WHAT YOU CONSISTENTLY TALK ABOUT

This becomes what the organization values. If you constantly ask about metrics and results, the organization will focus on metrics and results.

If you regularly ask about people's well-being and development, the organization will value people's well-being and development.

I made it a practice to start every team meeting by celebrating someone's contribution or achievement. Sometimes it was a major project completion. Sometimes it was someone going above and beyond to help a school. Sometimes it was creative problem-solving or excellent customer service.

This consistent communication pattern created a culture of recognition and appreciation. Team members started recognizing each other. People knew their contributions mattered and would be noticed.

HOW YOU RESPOND TO PROBLEMS

This signals what behavior is acceptable. If people are punished for admitting mistakes, they'll hide mistakes. If they are thanked for surfacing problems early, they'll bring you problems early.

When team members came to me with problems they had caused—a mistake, an oversight, a poor decision—my response was consistent: "Thank you for telling me. Let's figure out how to fix this and what we can learn from it."

This created a culture where problems were addressed quickly rather than hidden until they became crises.

WHAT YOU CELEBRATE

This becomes what people strive for.

- Celebrate innovation, and people will innovate.
- Celebrate rule-following, and people will follow rules.
- Celebrate customer service, and people will serve customers well.

I made sure to publicly celebrate not just successful outcomes, but also the behaviors and values I wanted to see more of, like collaboration, creative problem-solving, going beyond the minimum, supporting colleagues, and serving our schools with excellence.

Growing The Skillset

Communication is not simply a tool; it's the primary instrument of leadership. Everything you accomplish as a leader happens through communication.

- You cast vision through communication.
- You build trust through communication.
- You develop people through communication.
- You navigate change through communication.
- You resolve conflict through communication.
- You create culture through communication.

Invest in becoming an exceptional communicator. Study it. Practice it. Seek feedback on it. Refine it continuously. The return on that investment will be extraordinary.

Remember that effective communication integrates military precision with servant leadership empathy. Be clear, be complete, be consistent, and also listen deeply, adapt thoughtfully, and connect authentically.

Your people are listening to what you say and how you say it.

- They're watching what you communicate about and what you ignore.
- They're noting when you communicate and when you're silent.
- They're learning from your example.

Communicate with intention. Communicate with integrity. Communicate with excellence.

DEVELOPING COMMUNICATION SKILLS

Communication skills can be developed and improved with intentional practice:

- **Seek feedback**: Ask trusted colleagues, mentors, or team members questions like, "How effective is my communication? What could I do better?" Then, be specific. "Was that briefing clear?" "Did my email make sense?" "How did that difficult conversation feel from your perspective?"
- **Record and review**: Record yourself giving presentations or leading meetings (with permission). Watch or listen to the recordings. You'll notice verbal tics, unclear explanations, or missed opportunities you didn't catch in the moment.
- **Study great communicators**: Pay attention to leaders who communicate effectively. What do they do? How do they structure messages? How do they handle questions? How do they adapt to different audiences?
- **Practice difficult conversations**: Role-play challenging conversations with a trusted friend or mentor. Practice delivering bad news, providing corrective feedback, or navigating conflict. Practice makes the real conversations easier.
- **Read about communication**: Find books, podcasts, and other resources to help improve how you communicate.

- **Join Toastmasters or similar organizations**: Practicing public speaking in a supportive environment builds skills and confidence.
- **Write regularly**: Writing forces clarity of thought. Start a leadership blog, write internal memos, or draft articles. The practice of organizing thoughts into written words improves all communication. Even if you don't share it with anyone, or only those closest to you at first, writing is a valuable tool.

Communication Mistakes to Avoid

Even experienced leaders make communication mistakes. Here are the most common ones and how to avoid them:

- **The assumption trap**: Assuming people know what you're thinking, what you want, or what's expected. Leaders often have information and context that their teams don't. What's obvious to you may not be obvious to them.
- **Solution**: Over-communicate expectations, context, and reasoning. What feels like repetition to you may be the first time someone is really hearing and understanding the message.

HINT INSTEAD OF HELP

Hinting at problems or concerns instead of addressing them directly often comes from a desire to be nice or avoid confrontation, but it creates confusion and doesn't solve problems.

- **Trying to be nice**: I once spent three weeks hinting to a team member that their project documentation needed improvement. I would say things like, "It would be great if we had more detailed docs," or "I wonder if users will understand this." Finally, someone asked me, "Have you told them their documentation is insufficient?"
- **Solution**: Be direct and clear, while remaining respectful. I hadn't been. I had hinted, hoped, and wished—but I hadn't communicated clearly. "I need you to improve the documentation on this project. Specifically, users need step-by-step instructions with screenshots. Can you have that completed by Friday?" Once I did, the problem was quickly solved.

THE EMAIL WAR

Trying to resolve conflict or complex issues via email. Email lacks tone, removes human connection, and often escalates rather than resolves tension.

- **Don't end up in a volley**: If an email exchange goes back and forth more than twice without resolution, it's time for a conversation. Makes for exciting tennis, but not effective communication.
- **Solution**: "This is important enough that we should talk in person. Can we meet at 2:00 PM today?"

THE SURPRISE ANNOUNCEMENT

Announcing major decisions that affect people without any warning or preparation. This destroys trust and creates resentment, even when the decision itself is good.

- **No blind-siding**: When I reorganized my department, I made sure to have individual conversations with affected team members before the public announcement.
- **Solution**: No one was surprised. Everyone had been consulted. The announcement was confirmation, not shock. If a decision affects someone, they should hear about it from you, directly, before any public announcement.

THE UNCLEAR EXPECTATION

Don't assign tasks or responsibilities without clear expectations about what success looks like, when it's due, or what priority it has.

- **Beating around the bush**: "Can you work on improving our network documentation?" is unclear. When should it be done? How detailed? What's the priority compared to other work? In contrast, "Can you create comprehensive network documentation for all our core switches, including configuration details and network diagrams, by the end of the month? This is your top priority after daily support tickets" is clear.
- **Solution**: Be specific about what, when, why, and how important.

THE FORGOT TO FOLLOW UP

Important messages need reinforcement, checking for understanding, and follow-up.

- **Once is not enough**: Communicating once and assuming the job is done doesn't cut it.

- **Solution**: Build follow-up into your communication plan. If you announce a change, check in a week later to see how implementation is going. If you provide feedback, check back to see if improvement is happening.

Putting It into Practice

Effective communication requires consistent daily practice. Here are practical ways to improve your communication.

- **This week**:

    - If you don't already have them, schedule one-on-ones with each of your direct reports.
    - Before your next meeting, write and distribute a clear agenda.
    - Before your next email, pause and consider. Is this the right channel? Could this be clearer? What action do I need?
    - Have one difficult conversation you've been avoiding.
    - Ask for feedback on your communication from someone you trust.

- **This month**:

    - Audit communication channels. Are you using the right ones? Over-relying on email? Having too many meetings?
    - Implement a regular communication rhythm. Daily huddle, weekly one-on-ones, and monthly team meeting.

- Record yourself giving a presentation or leading a meeting, then review it.
- Read one book on communication or have one conversation with a mentor about improving your skills.
- Create a communication plan for an upcoming change or initiative.

- **This quarter**:

  - Conduct a communication survey. Ask your team to rate your communication effectiveness and provide improvement suggestions.
  - Address your biggest communication weakness. Whether it's public speaking, written communication, difficult conversations, or something else.
  - Teach a class or give a presentation on something you know well. Teaching forces clarity.
  - Develop a communication template for recurring situations (project updates, change announcements, etc.).
  - Review and improve your team's communication norms and practices.

The Communication Commitment

Communication is not a skill mastered once and then forgotten. It's a daily practice that requires continuous attention and improvement. The best leaders are always working on communicating more clearly, more empathetically, and more effectively.

Commit to these communication principles:

- **I will communicate clearly**: I will use simple language, avoid jargon, and ensure my message is understood.
- **I will communicate completely**: I will provide all necessary information and context, not make people guess or assume.
- **I will communicate honestly**: I will tell the truth, admit when I don't know something, and acknowledge mistakes.
- **I will listen actively**: I will truly hear what people are saying, not just wait for my turn to talk.
- **I will adapt my message**: I will consider my audience and communicate in ways that resonate with them.
- **I will be consistent**: I will communicate regularly, not just when there's a crisis or problem.
- **I will follow up**: I will verify understanding, check on progress, and close communication loops.
- **I will keep improving**: I will seek feedback, learn from mistakes, and continuously develop my communication skills.

Communication is your essential tool as a leader. How well you use it will largely determine how effective you are in every other aspect of leadership. Invest in developing this skill. Practice it daily. Refine it continuously.

Your mission depends on it. Your people deserve it. Your leadership requires it.

Chapter 6

Adaptability: Leading Through Change

In the very early years of unmanned aerial vehicles (UAVs), our command wanted to see a live stream from a remote drone. That hadn't been done before in the environment we were in. The basic technology existed, but the integration didn't. Command staff needed to see it, intelligence analysts needed to see it, and they needed to see it simultaneously, which meant more than just a single monitor in a secure facility.

I saw two different responses to this problem. Some leaders simply reported that it couldn't be done. They looked at the existing systems, saw the limitations, and stopped there. "The feed system can't distribute. The distribution system can't receive the UAV signal. Neither has room for more than two or three people to view. It's impossible with what we have."

Other leaders looked at the same problem and saw possibilities. One team, led by a sergeant who understood both the mission need and the systems' capabilities, created a solution that had never been attempted before. They fabricated custom cables to bring the UAV stream from the system that could receive it to the system that could distribute it. They created another cable to send the stream to a large-screen TV in a tent outside the facility so that more people could view simultaneously. They configured systems in ways that had never been done before, effectively creating a new capability from existing equipment.

Within days, the command staff was watching live UAV feeds during mission briefs. Intelligence analysts could see real-time imagery. The capability that "couldn't be done" became standard operating procedure. That's adaptability in leadership, the ability to look beyond "this is how we've always done it" and ask "what does the mission require, and how can we make it happen?" Not by ignoring constraints, but by creatively working within them to accomplish what matters.

Years later, as a CIO, I faced a different but equally dramatic change. A global pandemic shut down schools overnight. Everything we knew about delivering education had to be reimagined in days, not months. The leaders who succeeded during both types of crisis shared a common trait: they could adapt without losing their center.

The Paradox of Adaptability

Here's what seems contradictory at first. The best adaptive leaders are also the most grounded in principles. They can change tactics rapidly because they're anchored to unchanging values. They know what must never change, which frees them to change everything else.

In the military, we called this "commander's intent." The specific plan might change as soon as contact with the enemy occurred, but the intent—what we were ultimately trying to accomplish and why—remained constant. Adaptable leaders communicate intent clearly, then empower their teams to adjust methods as circumstances demand.

The military units I served in understood this intuitively. Earlier than in the process-heavy, risk-averse cultures of some organizations, military leaders were expected to adapt to circumstances. The planning process emphasized branches and sequels, the host of alternative courses of action for when things didn't go as expected. Because things never go as expected.

Servant leadership adds an important dimension to adaptability: genuine concern for how change affects people. Adaptation isn't just about accomplishing the mission despite change; it's about helping your people navigate change successfully. The adaptive servant leader asks not only, "How do we accomplish the mission in this new environment?" but also, "How do I help my team succeed through this transition?"

Why Leaders Resist Adaptation

Before discussing how to become more adaptable, understanding why leaders resist change—even when they intellectually recognize its necessity—is required.

- **Ego and identity**: Many leaders tie their identity to their expertise. "I'm successful because I know how to do this." When the environment changes and that expertise becomes less relevant, it threatens their sense of self-worth. Admitting that old methods no longer work feels like admitting failure. I experienced this when I transitioned from network technician to CIO. My technical expertise—my identity as someone who could solve any network problem—was my identity. Suddenly, that mattered less than my ability to manage people, budgets, and strategy. I had to adapt not just my skills but my self-concept.

- **Fear of losing control**: Change introduces uncertainty. Leaders who need to feel in control at all times struggle with adaptation because they can't control all the variables during transitions. They'd rather stick with a suboptimal approach they can predict than try a better approach with uncertain outcomes.
- **Investment in current methods**: "We've always done it this way" isn't just stubbornness; it's recognition of the investment made in current systems. Adapting means that the time, energy, and resources spent developing current methods might be lost. Some leaders resist this sunk cost. Whenever I've taken on a leadership role, I've inherited systems and processes that the previous leadership had spent years implementing. Some worked well; some did not. Sometimes changing them meant acknowledging that all that effort had been misguided. That's hard.
- **Lack of psychological safety**: In organizations where mistakes are punished harshly, leaders become risk-averse. Adaptation requires experimentation, and experimentation produces failures. If the culture doesn't tolerate failure, leaders won't adapt until forced to, and by then it's often too late.
- **Misunderstanding what should stay constant**: Some leaders fail to distinguish between principles and methods. They resist changing methods because they mistakenly believe doing so means abandoning principles. This confusion makes them rigid when they should be flexible.

Understanding these resistance factors helps in two ways. First, you can identify and address them in yourself. Second, you can help team members work through their resistance to the changes you're leading.

The Foundations of Adaptive Leadership

Becoming an adaptive leader requires building specific capabilities and mindsets.

SITUATIONAL AWARENESS

You can't adapt to changes you don't see coming. Adaptive leaders develop keen situational awareness. They pay attention to weak signals that indicate shifts in the environment.

In the military, we called this "reading the battlefield." You noticed when enemy patterns changed, when local attitudes shifted, when your team's morale dipped. You paid attention to what was different today compared to yesterday.

In my technology leadership roles, I learned to watch for similar signals, like changing user behavior, emerging technologies, shifts in budget priorities, and staff energy levels. The leader who notices change early can adapt proactively; the leader who misses the signals adapts reactively, and that's usually too late.

Develop these practices:

- **Regular environmental scanning**: What's changing in the industry, organization, or team?
- **Diverse information sources**: Don't rely on filtered information from a single source.
- **Direct observation**: Get out of the office and see what's actually happening.

- **Listening to frontline perspectives**: The people closest to the work often see changes first.
- **Monitoring leading indicators**: What metrics predict future problems?

COMFORT WITH AMBIGUITY

Adaptive leaders can function effectively despite incomplete information and unclear situations. They're comfortable saying, "I don't know yet," while continuing to lead.

This doesn't mean they're indecisive. Rather, they can make provisional decisions based on available information, knowing such decisions might need revision as circumstances clarify. They distinguish between decisions that must be made now, as opposed to those that can wait for better information.

During the pandemic transition to remote learning, we faced dozens of decisions with incomplete information. Will schools be closed for weeks or months? Will families have internet access? Will teachers be able to adapt? We couldn't afford to wait for perfect information. We had to act on what we knew and adjust as we learned more.

LEARNING AGILITY

Adaptive leaders are aggressive learners. They seek out new information, experiment with new approaches, and extract lessons from both successes and failures.

When I transitioned from being a PSYOP NCO to a Signal Officer, I had to learn an entirely new role and branch of the Army. I couldn't rely on my previous expertise; I had to become a student again. That experience taught me that learning agility often matters more than existing knowledge.

Cultivate learning agility by:

- **Asking**: "What can I learn from this?" after every significant experience.
- **Seeking**: Feedback actively rather than defensively.
- **Reading**: Broadly outside your field.
- **Experimenting**: With new approaches in low-stakes situations.
- **Teaching**: What you're learning; teaching deepens understanding.

STRONG CORE VALUES

Paradoxically, the most adaptable leaders are those with the strongest core values. They can change tactics freely because they know what must never change.

Define leadership nonnegotiables. For me, these include:

- Clarity in all communications.
- Respect for every individual's dignity.
- Commitment to the mission.
- Responsibility for my team's welfare.
- Continuous improvement.

When circumstances force changes, I test potential adaptations against these values. If a new approach violates core values, I reject it—regardless of short-term benefits. If it's consistent with values, I'm free to experiment.

This clarity prevents "adaptation" from becoming aimless drift. You're not changing because change itself is good; you're adapting methods to better serve unchanging principles.

Practical Adaptation Strategies

How to actually lead through change? Here are strategies drawn from both military and civilian experience.

COMMUNICATE THE WHY BEFORE THE WHAT

When introducing change, leaders often start with the details, like "Here's the new process, here are the steps, here's the timeline." But people need to understand why before they can embrace how.

Start with the reason for change. What problem are you solving? What opportunity are you pursuing? What will be better after the change? Only after establishing the why do you move to the what and how.

When we transitioned to one-to-one devices, giving every student their own computer, we didn't start with technical specifications. We started with the educational why: equity of access, personalized learning, and preparing students for a digital world. Once teachers understood the purpose, they were more willing to navigate the challenges of implementation.

INVOLVE PEOPLE IN DESIGNING CHANGE

The best adaptations come from the people closest to the work. They understand the practical realities that distant leaders might miss. Moreover, people support changes they help create.

When the military units I was in needed to adapt tactics, our commander didn't lock himself in a room and design a new approach. He brought together people from different specialties and ranks, presented the problem, and asked for input. The solution we developed collectively was better than anything one person could have designed—and everyone was committed to making it work because they'd contributed to it.

As a CIO facing technology changes, I followed the same principle. When we needed to redesign our help desk processes, I involved the technicians. They knew what worked and what didn't. Their ideas were practical and implementable.

PILOT AND ITERATE

Rarely do you need to implement changes across an entire organization simultaneously. Instead, pilot new approaches with a small team, learn from the experience, adjust, then expand.

This reduces risk. If the adaptation doesn't work as planned, you've affected a small group rather than the entire organization. It also demonstrates success before asking others to change; seeing peers succeed makes people more willing to try.

When implementing new educational technologies, we always piloted with volunteer teachers first. They experimented, encountered problems, found solutions, and became advocates. When we expanded to the broader staff, we already had proven approaches and internal champions.

MAINTAIN WHAT WORKS

Adaptation doesn't mean changing everything. Identify what's working well and protect it during transitions. This provides stability and continuity while other factors change.

During major organizational changes, I always looked for the "keep doing" items alongside the "start doing" and "stop doing" items. "We're changing our ticketing system, but our commitment to responding to every request within four hours remains the same." This balance prevents change fatigue and reinforces core values.

PROVIDE SUPPORT DURING TRANSITIONS

Change is hard. Even beneficial changes create stress. Adaptive leaders recognize this and provide extra support during transitions. This might include:

- Additional training for developing new skills.
- More frequent communication and feedback.
- Temporary additional resources to handle both old and new responsibilities.
- Patience with mistakes during the learning period.
- Recognition of the effort required for the transition.

When teachers transitioned to remote learning during the pandemic, we provided daily support sessions, created peer learning groups, celebrated small successes, and explicitly acknowledged how hard the transition was. This support made the adaptation possible.

SET CLEAR SUCCESS METRICS

How will you know if the adaptation is working? Define success metrics before implementing change, then monitor them consistently.

These metrics should include both outcome measures (Did we accomplish the goal?) and process measures (Is the new approach sustainable?). Be willing to declare an adaptation unsuccessful and try something else if metrics show it's not working.

In one instance, after changing our technology procurement process, we tracked both efficiency metrics (time from request to delivery) and satisfaction metrics (user ratings of the new process). The data showed us what was working and what needed further adjustment.

Leading Different Types of Change

Not all changes are the same. Effective adaptive leaders adjust their approach based on the type of change they're facing.

CRISIS ADAPTATION

Sometimes change is urgent, with a crisis demanding immediate adaptation. In these situations:

- Make the best decision you can with the available information.
- Communicate clearly and frequently.
- Accept that the first solution might be temporary.
- Focus on immediate stability before long-term optimization.
- Forgive mistakes more readily during crisis response.

The pandemic school closure was very much a crisis adaptation. We couldn't wait for perfect solutions. We implemented what we could immediately, knowing we'd improve it later. The priority was maintaining educational continuity.

STRATEGIC ADAPTATION

Other changes are anticipated and planned. Strategic adaptations to emerging trends or opportunities provide more time for deliberate approaches:

- Conduct a thorough analysis of options.
- Involve stakeholders in planning.
- Design comprehensive implementation plans.
- Pilot before full implementation.
- Build capability before demanding performance.

Our school district IT team understood that cloud-based systems would eventually replace on-premise servers, so we had time to plan the transition strategically. We piloted solutions, trained staff, migrated systems in logical phases, and managed the change deliberately over several years.

CULTURAL ADAPTATION

Some changes require shifting organizational culture, the beliefs, values, and norms that guide behavior. This is the slowest and most difficult adaptation. It requires:

- Clear articulation of desired culture.
- Modeling new behaviors consistently at leadership levels.
- Aligning systems and processes with culture.
- Recognizing and celebrating cultural shifts when they appear.
- Patience, culture changes slowly.

Shifting from a "technology serves IT" mindset to a "IT serves education" mindset in a school district required cultural adaptation. We had to change not just what we did but how we thought about our purpose. That can take years of consistent messaging, behavior modeling, and system alignment.

Personal Adaptability: Leading Your Own Change

Before you can lead organizational adaptation, you must be personally adaptable. This requires honest self-assessment and intentional development.

DON'T ADAPT CORE VALUES

The fundamental principles should remain constant. If a change would require violating integrity, abandoning responsibility to people, or compromising ethical standards, don't adapt—resist.

I've seen leaders justify unethical behavior as "adapting to reality." That's not adaptation; it's rationalization. True adaptive leaders find ways to accomplish the mission that align with their values, even when that's harder.

DON'T ADAPT TO TEMPORARY FLUCTUATIONS

Some changes are permanent shifts that require adaptation. Others are temporary fluctuations that should be weathered rather than accommodated. Distinguish between:

- Trends (sustained directional changes) and fads (temporary enthusiasms).
- Structural changes (fundamental shifts) and situational changes (temporary conditions).
- Signal (meaningful information) and noise (random variation).

Overreacting to temporary fluctuations creates instability. Sometimes the best leadership decision is to maintain course despite short-term pressure to change.

DON'T ADAPT WHEN CONSISTENCY IS CRITICAL

In some domains, consistency matters more than optimization. Disciplinary processes, safety protocols, and ethical standards often fall into this category.

As a company commander, I maintained consistent standards for discipline even when circumstances changed. Soldiers needed to know what was expected of them regardless of the situation. Adapting standards to circumstances would have destroyed trust and order.

Similarly, in technology leadership, I maintained consistent security practices even when they were inconvenient. Security isn't a domain where adaptation to user preference is appropriate.

Building an Adaptive Organization

Personal adaptability matters, but your greatest impact comes from building organizational adaptability, in creating teams and systems that can change effectively.

HIRE FOR LEARNING AGILITY

When selecting team members, value learning agility as much as current expertise. The person who learns quickly will adapt to new circumstances. The person who relies solely on existing knowledge will struggle when that knowledge becomes obsolete.

Ask candidates to:

- Explain a time they had to learn something completely new.
- How they responded when their expertise wasn't sufficient.
- Describe a situation where they had to change their approach.
- The most recent skill they have developed.

Their answers will reveal whether they're adaptive learners or fixed in their expertise.

CREATE PSYCHOLOGICAL SAFETY

People adapt when they feel safe to experiment, fail, and learn. Create an environment where:

- Intelligent failures are learning opportunities, not career enders.
- Questions are welcomed, not punished.
- Admitting, "I don't know," is acceptable.
- Trying new approaches is encouraged.
- Feedback focuses on improvement, not blame.

In such environments, adaptation happens naturally because people aren't paralyzed by fear of failure.

DECENTRALIZE DECISION-MAKING

Organizations adapt faster when people at all levels can make decisions. Centralized, hierarchical decision-making creates bottlenecks that slow response to change.

Empower the people closest to the work to adapt methods within clear guidelines. Define the boundaries of their authority, communicate intent clearly, then trust them to adjust tactics as circumstances demand.

This was the LGOPs philosophy in action—small groups making decisions to support the overall mission without waiting for higher headquarters to tell them what to do.

BUILD DIVERSE TEAMS

Homogeneous teams adapt poorly because everyone sees situations similarly. Diverse teams in background, experience, perspective, and thinking styles generate more adaptive solutions.

When facing change, diverse teams consider more possibilities and catch blind spots that homogeneous groups miss. Deliberately build teams with different perspectives and create processes that surface those differences productively.

MAINTAIN ORGANIZATIONAL LEARNING

Adaptive organizations capture and share learning. They conduct after-action reviews, document lessons learned, and ensure knowledge gained from one adaptation benefits future situations.

After every major project or change initiative, we conducted formal reviews asking:

- What did we expect to happen?
- What actually happened?
- Why was there a difference?
- What will we do differently next time?

Such systematic learning made each subsequent adaptation easier and more successful.

The Discipline of Continuous Adaptation

Ultimately, adaptability isn't a one-time capability; it's a continuous discipline to practice. The environment keeps changing, the organization keeps evolving, and your capabilities keep developing.

The adaptive leader commits to:

- **Regular environmental scanning**: Continuously monitoring for changes that might require adaptation.
- **Ongoing learning**: Always developing new capabilities and understanding.
- **Systematic experimentation**: Regularly testing new approaches in controlled ways.
- **Honest assessment**: Periodically evaluating what's working and what isn't.
- **Courageous adjustment**: Changing course when evidence suggests current approaches aren't optimal.

This discipline ensures you're adapting proactively rather than reactively, leading change rather than being overwhelmed by it.

ASSESS YOUR ADAPTABILITY

Ask yourself:

- How do I typically respond when plans change?
- Do I see change as threat or opportunity?
- Can I admit when my previous approach isn't working?
- Do I seek out new learning or rely on existing expertise?
- How comfortable am I with ambiguity?
- Do I encourage experimentation or demand proven methods?

The answers reveal where you're naturally adaptive and where you need to grow.

DELIBERATELY PRACTICE ADAPTATION

Like any skill, adaptability improves with practice. Create opportunities to adapt in lower-stakes situations:

- Try new approaches to routine tasks.
- Learn skills outside your expertise area.
- Work with people from different backgrounds.
- Travel to unfamiliar places.
- Read perspectives that challenge your assumptions.
- Take on projects with uncertain outcomes.

These experiences build adaptation muscles, making you more capable when high-stakes changes occur.

BUILD RESILIENCE

Adaptation requires resilience, which is the ability to handle stress and setbacks without breaking. Build it through:

- Strong relationships that provide support during difficult changes.
- Physical health practices that maintain energy.
- Reflection practices that process experiences and emotions.
- Sense of purpose that transcends current circumstances.
- Having a growth mindset that views challenges as development opportunities.

The most adaptable leaders I've known, in combat and in corporate settings, were also the most resilient. They could handle the stress of change because they'd built the capacity to recover from setbacks.

Adaptation in Action: Real-World Case Studies

Let me share detailed stories that illustrate adaptive leadership in both military and civilian contexts. These aren't theoretical; they're situations where adaptation made the difference between success and failure.

THE PANDEMIC TECHNOLOGY PIVOT

When schools shut down in March 2020 due to COVID-19, I was the CIO of a large school district with about 40,000 students. We had to transition from in-person education to remote learning in less than a week. It was the most dramatic change I'd ever led in civilian life.

My initial instinct was to solve this with technology. We needed devices for students, internet connectivity, video conferencing tools, and learning management systems. I started developing a comprehensive technology deployment plan.

Then I stopped and asked, "What problem are we really solving?" The problem wasn't technology. It was educational continuity. Technology was a tool, but the real challenge was helping teachers teach and students learn in an entirely new environment. That reframing changed everything.

Instead of leading with a technology solution, we convened a cross-functional team of teachers, principals, parents, students, IT staff, and curriculum specialists. We presented the challenge, "We need to maintain educational engagement with students who can't come to school. How do we do that?"

The solutions that emerged were more holistic than my initial technology-focused approach. Yes, we needed devices and connectivity, but we also needed:

- Simple, consistent tools that teachers could learn quickly.
- Support systems for teachers who'd never taught online.
- Engagement strategies for students who struggled with remote learning.
- Equity considerations for students without home support.
- Mental health resources for everyone under enormous stress.
- Communication plans to keep parents informed.
- Flexibility to adapt as we learned what worked.

We implemented in phases. Week one was basic connectivity, just getting everyone able to communicate. Then we added structure, with regular schedules and expectations. Over time, quality improved. We found better tools and teaching strategies. Through it all, we focused on engagement and reaching students who were struggling.

Each week, we assessed what was working and what wasn't. We made rapid adjustments based on feedback from teachers, students, and parents. We celebrated small successes and learned from failures without blame.

The technology team's role evolved. Instead of being solution providers ("Here's the tool, let me know if you have problems"), we became support partners ("What do you need to accomplish, and how can we help?"). That shift from technology-centered to user-centered made our adaptation successful.

Later, when we returned to in-person learning, we'd fundamentally changed how we thought about technology in education. The forced adaptation had revealed better approaches, which we maintained even after the crisis ended. That's the mark of successful adaptation—you emerge stronger than before, not just back to where you were.

AN AIRBORNE DIVISION'S RAPID DEPLOYMENT CAPABILITY

During my time with the 82nd Airborne, our core capability was rapid deployment; being ready to deploy anywhere in the world within eighteen hours. This required extreme adaptability because we never knew where we'd go or what mission we'd face.

The division's approach to adaptation was systematic:

- **Rigorous core standards**: Certain fundamentals never changed, such as physical fitness, weapons proficiency, basic airborne skills, and small unit tactics. These were drilled constantly until they were instinctive.

- **Flexible mission training**: Beyond the core, training adapted to anticipated missions. If intelligence suggested we might deploy to a desert environment, we'd train for desert operations. If the mission profile shifted to urban terrain, we'd adjust our training focus.
- **Decentralized problem-solving**: The LGOPs philosophy meant that small units could adapt to local conditions without waiting for orders from higher headquarters. Squad leaders were trained to assess situations and make decisions that supported the overall mission.
- **Systematic after-action reviews**: After every training exercise or mission, we conducted detailed reviews. What worked? What didn't? What surprised us? What will we change next time? This ensured organizational learning.
- **Cross-training and redundancy**: Personnel were cross-trained so the unit could adapt to personnel losses. If a communications specialist were injured, someone else could perform those critical functions at a basic level.

This systematic approach to adaptability meant that, when unexpected situations arose—and they always did—the division could respond effectively. It wasn't chaos; it was disciplined flexibility.

I've applied this same framework in civilian technology leadership:

- Maintain core competencies that never change (service, security, ethics).
- Adapt specific initiatives to emerging needs and technologies.
- Empower teams to solve problems without always escalating to leadership.
- Conduct regular reviews to capture learning.
- Cross-train staff so the organization isn't vulnerable to single points of failure.

The framework works because it balances stability and change appropriately.

Adaptive Leadership Through Organizational Life Cycles

Organizations go through predictable life cycles, and adaptive leaders recognize that what works in one phase may not work in another. Your leadership approach must evolve as the organization matures.

STARTUP/FOUNDING PHASE

In the beginning, organizations need:

- Rapid decision-making with incomplete information.
- High tolerance for experimentation and failure.
- Flexibility in roles and processes.
- Intense focus on proving the concept.
- Personal relationships over formal systems.

In this phase, adaptive leaders move fast, try things, learn quickly, and pivot frequently. Formal processes would slow things down; structure would constrain necessary flexibility.

GROWTH PHASE

As organizations grow, they need:

- Documented processes to maintain consistency.
- Clear roles and responsibilities.

- Training systems to onboard new people.
- Scalable solutions rather than heroic individual efforts.
- Balance between innovation and stability.

Adaptive leaders recognize when informal approaches that worked with five people won't work with fifty. You need to add structure without losing the entrepreneurial energy that made you successful.

This transition is difficult. People who thrived in the startup phase sometimes resist the structure needed for growth. "We're losing what made us special," they complain. The adaptive leader helps them see that evolution isn't betrayal; it's necessary for continued success.

MATURITY PHASE

Mature organizations need:

- Optimized processes for efficiency.
- Clear accountability and metrics.
- Risk management and compliance systems.
- Succession planning and knowledge transfer.
- Strategic focus on sustaining competitive advantage.

Adaptive leaders in mature organizations must prevent petrification of systems, with processes designed to create efficiency rather than rigidity. The challenge is maintaining the benefits of maturity (stability, efficiency, predictability) while retaining the ability to innovate and change.

DECLINE OR RENEWAL PHASE

Organizations that fail to adapt eventually decline. At this point, they need:

- Honest assessment of what's not working.
- Willingness to abandon previously successful approaches.
- Courage to make difficult changes.
- Focus on core mission and values.
- Either significant adaptation or managed decline.

I've seen military units and civilian organizations reach this point. The adaptive leader recognizes decline early and drives renewal before a crisis makes it unavoidable. Sometimes this means returning to founding principles while shedding accumulated baggage. Sometimes it means reinventing the organization's purpose for a changed environment.

The key insight is that effective leadership looks different at various organizational stages. The adaptive leader recognizes which phase the organization is in and adjusts their approach accordingly. What made you successful in one phase may cause failure in the next if you don't adapt.

The Adaptive Leader's Daily Practice

Adaptability isn't just about responding to major changes; it's proactively built through daily practices that keep you flexible and responsive. Here are some specific habits that adaptive leaders cultivate.

START EACH DAY WITH OPEN QUESTIONS

- What's different today from yesterday?
- What assumption am I making that might not be true?
- Where am I resisting something that deserves consideration?
- What's one small experiment I could run today?

These questions create a mindset of curiosity rather than certainty, making you more receptive to signals that change is needed.

PRACTICE "YES, AND" THINKING

When someone proposes a new idea or points out a problem with current approaches, your first instinct might be "Yes, but …" This defensive response protects current methods, but blocks adaptation.

Instead, practice "Yes, and …" thinking:

- "Yes, that's a concern, *and* how might we address it?"
- "Yes, that's different from our current approach, *and* what could we learn by trying it?"
- "Yes, that will be challenging, *and* what would make it possible?"

This doesn't mean accepting every idea uncritically. It means staying open-minded long enough to understand before judging.

SEEK DISCONFIRMING INFORMATION

We naturally notice information that confirms our existing beliefs. Adaptive leaders deliberately seek information that contradicts their assumptions.

Ask yourself, "If I'm wrong about this, where would I see evidence?" Then look for that evidence. If you find it, you've identified something that needs to adapt. If you don't find it, you've strengthened your confidence that the current approach is sound.

REFLECT DAILY ON WHAT YOU LEARNED

At the end of each day, spend five minutes reflecting:

- What surprised me today?
- What didn't work as I expected?
- What did I learn that might change how I approach tomorrow?
- What feedback did I receive, and what does it suggest?

This daily reflection turns experience into learning, which enables adaptation.

MODEL ADAPTATION PUBLICLY

When you change your mind based on new information, say so explicitly, "I thought X, but after learning Y, I now think Z." This demonstrates that adaptation is a strength, not a weakness. It gives teams permission to adapt their own thinking.

Too many leaders hide their adaptation process, creating the illusion that they were always right. This makes others reluctant to adapt because it looks like admitting mistakes were made. Model the process openly.

Adaptation and Innovation: The Critical Connection

Adaptability and innovation are related but distinct. Innovation is creating something new; adaptation is responding effectively to change. The adaptive leader excels at both.

Innovation without adaptation fails because it doesn't respond to real needs or changing circumstances. Adaptation without innovation fails because it only reacts to changes others have initiated rather than shaping the future.

The adaptive leader asks both:

- **Adaptation**: "How should we respond to changes we're seeing?"
- **Innovation**: "What changes should we initiate to create better futures?"

In my technology leadership roles, I balanced:

- **Responding to the pandemic**: Adapting our infrastructure to support remote learning.
- **Shaping the future**: Innovating new approaches to professional development that would serve us beyond the crisis.

The most successful adaptations often include innovative elements—new solutions to new problems—rather than just old solutions in new circumstances.

Leading Adaptation Across Cultures

If you work in multicultural environments, as I did in Korea and Iraq, it becomes apparent that cultures vary in how they approach change and adaptation.

Some cultures value stability and tradition highly. Proposing rapid change can feel disrespectful of accumulated wisdom. In these contexts, adaptive leaders:

- Connect changes to traditional values.
- Move more slowly to build consensus.
- Honor what's being preserved even as some things change.
- Involve respected elders or senior leaders in designing adaptations.

Other cultures embrace change and innovation enthusiastically. In these contexts, maintaining necessary stability can be challenging. Adaptive leaders:

- Emphasize the principles that remain constant.
- Channel innovative energy toward strategic priorities.
- Celebrate both innovation and, where it serves the mission, consistency.

There's no single right approach to adaptation—context matters. The adaptive leader reads the cultural context and adjusts their approach accordingly. That's meta-adaptation: adapting your adaptation style to fit the situation.

Building a Personal Adaptation Plan

Becoming more adaptable requires intentional effort. A practical framework for developing your adaptive capacity includes the following.

MONTHLY ENVIRONMENTAL SCAN

Set aside time each month to assess the environment:

- What's changing in your industry or field?
- What's changing in your organization?
- What's changing with your team?
- What's changing in the broader world that might affect your work?
- What assumptions am I making that might no longer be true?

Document observations. Over time, patterns emerge that will help you anticipate changes before they become crises.

QUARTERLY ADAPTATION REVIEW

Every quarter, assess current approaches:

- What am I doing that's working well and should continue?
- What am I doing that's working but could work better with modification?
- What am I doing that's no longer effective and should stop?
- What am I not doing that I should start?

Based on this review, identify two or three specific adaptations to implement in the coming quarter. Keep the list short and focused; trying to change everything at once leads to changing nothing effectively.

ANNUAL LEARNING GOALS

Each year, identify specific capabilities to develop:

- What skill would make me more effective if I had it?
- What knowledge gap limits my effectiveness?
- What experience would broaden my perspective?
- What relationship would increase my understanding of a different context?

Create a concrete plan to develop that capability. Take a course, read specific books, seek out a mentor, take on a stretch assignment, or shadow someone with the skill you want to develop.

REGULAR FEEDBACK LOOPS

Create systematic ways to get feedback on your effectiveness:

- After-action reviews following major initiatives.
- Regular one-on-ones with team members who can share observations.
- Annual 360-degree feedback assessments.
- Customer or stakeholder satisfaction surveys.
- Mentor conversations about your development.

Don't just collect feedback. Analyze it for patterns and act on what you learn. The adaptive leader sees feedback as information for improvement, not judgment on worth.

EXPERIMENTATION PRACTICE

Deliberately practice adaptation by experimenting with new approaches in low-stakes situations:

- Try a new method for conducting meetings.
- Experiment with different communication styles.
- Test alternative approaches to routine tasks.
- Learn a new tool or technology.
- Work with someone from a different background.

Small experiments will build confidence and capability for larger adaptations when they're needed.

The Adaptation Journey Continues

Reading about adaptation doesn't make you adaptive any more than reading about fitness makes you fit. Adaptability develops through practice via facing changes and working through them, experimenting with new approaches while learning from the results, and helping others navigate transitions to discover what works.

Your adaptation journey is ongoing. Start where you are. Pick one practice from this chapter and implement it this week. Conduct an environmental scan. Try a new approach to a routine task. Seek feedback from someone who sees your blind spots. Reflect on what surprised you today.

Small adaptations compound over time into significant capability. The leader who adapts a little each day becomes dramatically more capable moving forward. The leader who resists all small adaptations eventually faces crisis-level change they're unprepared to handle.

The environment will keep changing. Technology will continue evolving. Organizations will face new challenges. The leaders who thrive, who help their teams and organizations thrive, will be those who maintain strong values while adapting their methods to emerging realities. They'll be leaders who understand that adaptation isn't abandoning your principles; it's finding new ways to live them out in changing circumstances.

The world needs leaders who can adapt without losing their center, who can change tactics without compromising values, who can help others navigate change while maintaining what matters most. Adaptive servant leaders who put mission first and people always, no matter how much the circumstances change.

True adaptive leadership is about maintaining core purpose and values while continuously adjusting methods to serve them better in changing circumstances. It's about being grounded enough in principles that you're free to be flexible in practice.

The most effective leaders I've known—military or corporate, in crisis situations or stable environments—have all been adaptive. They could read their environment, recognize when change was needed, help others through transitions, and emerge stronger from the experience.

They understood that the world keeps changing, and leaders must change with it. Not by abandoning who they are, but by finding new ways to express their values and accomplish their mission in new realities.

That's the kind of leader our organizations need. That's the kind of leader our world needs. And with intentional practice, that's the kind of leader you can become.

Chapter 7

Develop Future Leaders: The Legacy of Leadership

Any time I get ready to leave a job, position, or other leadership role, I ask myself, "What will remain after I leave?"

In the military, we normally think about the operations we'd conducted, the missions we'd supported. In the civilian world, we think about the products we've developed and the institutional change we've made.

But all that ends when you walk out the door, while the people you've trained, the soldiers you've mentored, the other leaders you've developed remain. They'll train others and lead missions and projects you'll never hear about. They'll make decisions based on what you taught them. *That's* your legacy. *That's* what remains.

Years after I've left positions, I receive messages from soldiers I served with, telling me about their promotions, assignments, and leadership challenges. Employees I worked with have contacted me about things they're working on, challenges they're facing, and more. The leaders I'd helped develop were still serving, still leading, still making a difference.

This is the paradox of leadership development. Your greatest achievement as a leader is creating leaders who surpass you.

The Coaching Tree: Lessons from the NFL

The true power of leadership development reveals itself across generations. When helping develop a leader who develops other leaders, who then develop still more leaders, your impact multiplies exponentially across time and organizations.

One of the most visible examples of leadership development's ripple effect is professional football. NFL analysts frequently discuss "coaching trees," the network of successful coaches who trace their development back to a single mentor. These illustrate how intentional leadership development compounds over time.

Consider Bill Walsh, who coached the San Francisco 49ers from 1979 to 1988. Walsh didn't just win three Super Bowls; he deliberately developed assistant coaches who would carry his principles forward. His coaching tree includes over twenty head coaches and numerous coordinators who went on to build their own successful programs.

But the tree didn't stop there. Mike Holmgren learned under Walsh, then developed coaches like Andy Reid and Jon Gruden. Reid, in turn, mentored coaches like Doug Pederson, who won a Super Bowl with the Philadelphia Eagles, and Matt Nagy. The ripple extends across decades and multiple generations.

What made Walsh's tree so productive wasn't just his tactical brilliance; it was his systematic approach to developing leaders:

- **He gave assistants real responsibility**: Walsh delegated play-calling and game-planning responsibilities to coordinators, allowing them to develop decision-making skills in high-pressure situations. He didn't micromanage; he mentored through the process.

- **He taught principles, not just plays**: Walsh emphasized the "why" behind every decision. His assistants didn't just memorize a playbook; they understood the philosophy that produced it. When they became head coaches, they could adapt those principles to different personnel and situations.
- **He created a culture of teaching**: Everyone on Walsh's staff was expected to develop others, such as position coaches mentoring players who would later become coaches. This culture of development became self-perpetuating.
- **He stayed connected to his tree**: Walsh remained available to his former assistants throughout their careers, offering advice during critical moments. The relationship didn't end when they left his staff.

The contrast with other successful coaches is instructive. Some highly successful coaches produced very small coaching trees. They won games, but they didn't systematically develop future leaders. Their success died with their tenure because they focused exclusively on immediate results rather than building leadership capacity.

The coaching tree phenomenon demonstrates three critical truths about leadership development:

- **Developed leaders multiply impact far beyond their direct sphere of influence**: Walsh influenced not only the 49ers but dozens of NFL franchises over multiple decades. The principles he taught in the 1980s are still shaping NFL offenses today through coaches who never met him personally but learned from those he developed.
- **Leadership development takes intentional systems**: More is at play than just good intentions. Walsh created deliberate structures like assistant coaches' meetings, film study sessions, and delegation of responsibilities that developed leaders. It wasn't accidental; it was engineered.

- **Leadership legacy is long-term**: It is measured by who people become, not just what they accomplish under your watch. Walsh's true legacy isn't his three Super Bowl rings; it's the dozens of successful coaches who built winning programs using principles he taught them.

This pattern exists beyond football. Steve Jobs developed leaders at Apple who went on to lead companies like Disney and Tesla. General George Marshall's systematic development of Army officers during World War II produced leaders who shaped military and civilian institutions for decades. Warren Buffett's approach to developing investment managers at Berkshire Hathaway has produced multiple successful fund managers and business leaders.

A question for leaders is, "Are you building a coaching tree?" Twenty years from now, will there be leaders throughout your industry or organization who trace their development back to time spent on your team? Will they be implementing principles you taught them and developing the next generation using methods they learned from you?

That's the ultimate measure of leadership development; not just the immediate results your team achieves, but the compounding impact of leaders you've developed, which creates ripples that extend far beyond your direct influence.

This perspective should fundamentally change how you think about leadership development. You're not just developing individuals; you're planting seeds that will produce forests.

Why Leaders Fail to Develop Leaders

Despite universal agreement that developing future leaders is important, most organizations fail at it systematically. Having observed leadership development efforts across military and civilian contexts, I've identified several common failure points.

THE PRODUCTIVITY TRAP

Most leaders face constant pressure to deliver immediate results. Training someone takes time, which could be spent accomplishing tasks yourself. When I was a network technician, I watched our small team constantly firefighting technology problems. The most senior techs could fix issues faster than any of us. So, they did. For years.

The result? We never developed expertise. We remained dependent on them. When they left, the team struggled because no one had been systematically developed to operate at this level. They had maximized short-term productivity at the cost of long-term capability.

In the military, I often saw the opposite approach. Senior NCOs deliberately gave junior leaders challenging assignments, even when the senior leaders could have completed them faster and better. They invested time in brief backs, rehearsals, and after-action reviews (AARs). They sacrificed some short-term efficiency for long-term capability development.

The result? When those junior leaders faced difficult situations in Iraq and Afghanistan, they were ready. The investment in development paid dividends when it mattered most.

THE INSECURITY FACTOR

Some leaders resist developing strong subordinates because of insecurity. They fear being surpassed, replaced, or shown up. This fear is particularly common among leaders who rose through technical expertise rather than leadership ability.

When I transitioned from the military to civilian technology leadership, I encountered this repeatedly. Technical managers who had been promoted because they were excellent technicians often struggled to develop their teams. Their identity was built on being the smartest person in the room. Developing subordinates who might become more capable felt threatening.

Servant leadership directly confronts this insecurity. If your purpose is to serve others' growth, then their success becomes your success. When people surpass you, you've succeeded at your mission.

THE "THEY'RE NOT READY" EXCUSE

Perhaps the most insidious barrier to development is the belief that people need to be "ready" before you invest in developing them. Leaders wait for subordinates to demonstrate readiness before giving them developmental opportunities, but those opportunities are precisely what develop readiness.

This creates a catch-22. People can't prove they're ready without opportunities, but they won't get opportunities until they prove they're ready.

I fell into this trap early in my career as an NCO. I had inherited a team with varying skill levels. Some were strong performers; others struggled. I invested my development efforts primarily in the strong performers, reasoning that they had the most potential. I gave the struggling performers routine tasks while I waited for them to "step up."

It was a mentor who pointed out my error. "You're investing in people who would probably develop anyway," he said. "What about the others? Have you really invested in developing them, or have you just given up on them?"

He was right. I had written off several team members without truly investing in their development. When I changed approaches, providing structured development opportunities, coaching, and progressively challenging assignments, several of those "struggling" soldiers became strong contributors.

The military doesn't have the luxury of waiting for people to be ready. You develop the soldiers you have, not the soldiers you wish you had. This necessity creates more effective development systems.

THE LONG VIEW

Developing future leaders requires patience. Results aren't immediate. You invest time, energy, and resources today for benefits that may not materialize for years.

This long-term perspective runs counter to most organizational cultures, which emphasize quarterly results, annual performance cycles, and short-term wins. It requires leaders who can balance immediate operational demands with long-term capability building.

When I left my position as CIO after several years, I saw the power of leadership development. The operations I'd overseen were quickly forgotten, the systems I'd implemented replaced by newer ones, and the projects I'd led became historical footnotes.

But the leaders I'd developed endured. Some took senior positions in other organizations. Others advanced within our own organization. Several reached out to tell me how something I'd taught them had helped them navigate a difficult situation. Two became CIOs and developed their own team of future leaders.

That's legacy. That's what remains.

The Foundations of Leadership Development

Developing future leaders requires intentional systems, not random acts of mentoring. Based on my experience across both military and civilian contexts, effective leadership development rests on several foundations.

DEVELOPMENT IS A PRIMARY MISSION

In most organizations, development is something leaders do "when they have time," which means it rarely happens systematically. In effective organizations, development is recognized as a primary mission, equal in importance to operational tasks.

When I was in a training company in the Army, development wasn't a secondary mission; it was *the* mission. Every operational decision was filtered through the question, "How does this develop our soldiers and leaders?"

Later, in civilian leadership, I applied the same principle. We established that part of every leader's time would be dedicated to development activities, like coaching sessions, training delivery, mentoring meetings, and leadership development projects. This wasn't time "left over" after operational tasks; it was protected time, as important as any other meeting on the calendar.

This required saying no to some operational demands. It meant occasionally delivering results more slowly because we were using assignments as developmental opportunities. But it built a team that became progressively more capable.

PROGRESSIVE CHALLENGE

People develop through progressively challenging experiences, not through repetition of tasks they've already mastered. Effective development requires deliberately stretching people beyond their current comfort zone, but not so far that they break.

In the military, this is formalized through progressive assignments and training. A new lieutenant commands a platoon before commanding a company. An NCO leads a team before leading a squad, then a squad before leading a platoon. Each level provides challenges that stretch current capabilities while building toward the next level.

In my civilian technology leadership, I tried to replicate this progression. A help desk technician might lead a small project before taking on a larger one. A network technician might represent the department at a committee before leading it. A manager might oversee a vendor relationship before taking on an entire budget.

The key is making the stretch intentional and supported. Don't throw someone into deep water to see if they can swim; progressively deepen the water while teaching them to swim.

FAILURE AS A LEARNING TOOL

The military has an institutional commitment to learning from failure that most civilian organizations lack. After every significant operation or training event, the military conducts an AAR, a structured process for extracting lessons learned.

The AAR process is built on several principles:

- Everyone participates, regardless of rank.
- The focus is on learning, not blame.
- Both successes and failures are examined.
- Lessons are documented and shared.

When I led a technology department, we adopted this practice. After every major project, system implementation, or significant incident, we conducted an AAR. Initially, people were defensive because they feared the process was about assigning blame. Over time, they recognized it as a genuine learning and improvement opportunity.

This cultural shift was crucial. Instead of hiding failures or deflecting responsibility, people began openly discussing what went wrong and why. This honesty accelerated learning and development across the entire team.

COACHING AND FEEDBACK

Development requires regular, honest feedback delivered in a coaching context. Most organizations provide feedback far too infrequently. Annual performance reviews are too slow for effective development.

In the military, from my earliest assignment as a private in Korea to my last as a company commander, I experienced a counseling system. Squad leaders counseled team leaders monthly. Platoon sergeants counseled squad leaders monthly. This regular rhythm created multiple opportunities to provide feedback, adjust performance, and guide development.

As a civilian leader, I adopted a similar rhythm. Every team member had a regular one-on-one focused on development, not just task status. We discussed what they were learning, challenges they were facing, and skills they wanted to develop, including opportunities to do so.

These conversations were coaching sessions, not performance evaluations. The focus was forward-looking: "Where are you going?" "How can I help you get there?"

Measuring Leadership Development

One challenge in leadership development is measurement. How do you know if development efforts are working?

LEADING INDICATORS (SHORT-TERM)

Asking these questions will show if development efforts are happening, even before results are visible:

- **Time invested**: Are leaders spending time on developmental activities?
- **Participation rates**: Are people engaging with development opportunities?

- **Developmental conversations**: Are leaders having regular developmental conversations with their people?
- **Stretch assignments**: Are you creating and filling developmental stretch assignments?

PROGRESS INDICATORS (MEDIUM-TERM)

The answers to these questions show if people are developing, even before organizational results change:

- **Skill acquisition**: Are people demonstrating new capabilities?
- **Increased responsibility**: Are people taking on greater responsibility?
- **Leadership behaviors**: Are desired leadership behaviors increasing?
- **Problem-solving capability**: Are people solving more complex problems independently?

OUTCOME INDICATORS (LONG-TERM)

Answering these questions will show that development is producing organizational results:

- **Promotion rates**: Are people being promoted to leadership positions?
- **Internal fill rates**: When leadership positions open, are they being filled with internal candidates?
- **Succession depth**: For each critical position, are there two to three people who could step into it?
- **Organizational performance**: Are operational results improving?

- **Retention of high performers**: Are the best people staying?

LEGACY INDICATORS (VERY LONG-TERM)

These answers indicate lasting impact:

- **Alumni success**: Are people who leave the organization succeeding in leadership roles elsewhere?
- **Multi-generation development**: Are current leaders developing new ones effectively?
- **Cultural persistence**: Do leadership development practices continue after leadership changes?

The key is tracking multiple types of indicators. Leading indicators ensure you're doing the right activities. Progress indicators confirm that those activities are producing development. Outcome indicators show development is producing results. Legacy indicators reveal lasting impact.

Practical Development Methods

Leadership development isn't mysterious. It requires consistent application of proven methods.

DELIBERATE TASK ASSIGNMENT

Every task assignment is a development opportunity if approached intentionally. Instead of simply assigning work based on who can complete it most efficiently, consider who would benefit most from the developmental opportunity.

The key questions for developmental task assignment:

- What skill does this person need to develop next?
- What task would stretch them in that direction?
- How can I provide support without removing the challenge?
- What does success look like, and how will we know?

STRUCTURED MENTORING

Informal mentoring is valuable, but structured mentoring programs are more effective for systematic development. A structured approach ensures that mentoring relationships form intentionally, not randomly, and that they focus on clear developmental goals.

In the technology department, we implemented a structured mentoring program:

- **Developmental assessment**: Each team member identified two or three areas for development over the next year.
- **Mentor matching**: We connected people with mentors who had expertise in their development areas, which were not always their direct supervisors.
- **Structured meetings**: Mentor pairs met monthly with a loose agenda focusing on the mentee's developmental goals.
- **Periodic review**: Quarterly, we reviewed progress and adjusted developmental focus if needed.

This structure ensured that mentoring happened consistently, not just when people remembered or had time.

LEADERSHIP TRAINING

While experience is the best teacher, structured training accelerates development by providing frameworks, tools, and concepts that help people make sense of their experiences.

The military invests heavily in leadership education, like basic courses for junior leaders, advanced courses for mid-level leaders, and senior courses for executive level leaders. This education doesn't replace experience, but it provides conceptual frameworks that help leaders learn from experience more effectively.

Civilian organizations often can't afford military-style training programs, but we can create more modest alternatives:

- **Monthly leadership book discussions**: Select leadership books, read them individually, and discuss their application together.
- **Leadership topic workshops**: Quarterly half-day workshops on specific leadership topics, such as communication, conflict resolution, decision-making, etc.
- **Cross-department exchanges**: Partner with other departments to share leadership practices and learn from each other's approaches.
- **Conference attendance**: Send team members to regional and national conferences that focus on leadership and professional development.

This is a method that I've used with great success. The investment was modest. It was less than 2 percent of our budget, but the impact was significant. It was this development that helped create a cadre of teacher tech leaders who helped the district quickly make the transition from in-person to remote learning.

DELEGATION AS DEVELOPMENT

Delegation is often viewed as simply off-loading work, but properly executed, delegation is one of the most powerful development tools available:

- **Task delegation**: "Complete this spreadsheet and return it to me by Friday."
- **Developmental delegation**: "We need to analyze our network performance trends. I'd like you to determine what data we should collect, how to analyze it, and what recommendations we should make based on the results. Let's meet midweek to discuss your approach, and then you'll present findings to the leadership team next month."

Developmental delegation transfers not just tasks but also decision-making authority, problem-solving responsibility, and learning opportunities. It requires more initial investment from the leader, including defining the problem rather than the solution, coaching through the process, and accepting that the subordinate's approach might differ from your own.

For some leaders, one major challenge is learning to delegate the developmental framework. Their instinct is to define exactly how things should be done, based on their technical background. This approach developed task-completers, not leaders.

Over time, I've learned to delegate outcomes, not methods. "Here's the problem we need to solve and the constraints we're working within. How would you approach this?" This approach was initially slower and more frustrating, as people didn't always approach problems the way I would have. But it developed problem-solvers and leaders, not just task-executors.

Building a Development Culture

Individual development efforts matter, but organization-wide development cultures multiply impact. Several practices build such cultures.

MAKE DEVELOPMENT VISIBLE

In most organizations, development happens behind closed doors in private coaching sessions, confidential mentoring relationships, and individual training. While confidentiality has its place, making development visible sends powerful cultural messages.

Begin celebrating development milestones publicly:

- Announce when team members completed certifications or degrees.
- Highlight stretch assignments and new responsibilities in team meetings.
- Share lessons learned from failures in public forums.
- Recognize mentors who invested in others' development.

Such visibility communicates that development is valued, celebrated, and expected. It is not something people are expected to do quietly in their spare time.

REWARD THE DEVELOPMENT OF OTHERS

Most performance evaluation systems reward individual accomplishment. If you want leaders to develop others, you must explicitly reward them for doing so.

Some organizations have seen success when modifying performance evaluation criteria to include "development of others" as a primary factor, equal in weight to operational results. Leaders were evaluated not just on what they personally accomplished, but on how effectively they developed their team members.

This change shifted behavior noticeably. Leaders began viewing development as part of their job, not an optional "extra credit" score. They invested time in coaching, mentoring, and creating developmental opportunities because these activities were explicitly valued and rewarded.

CREATE DEVELOPMENTAL PATHWAYS

People develop more intentionally when they can see clear pathways forward. In the military, career progression is relatively transparent. You know what's required to advance to the next rank, what assignments prepare you for increased responsibility, and what training and education are expected.

Most civilian organizations lack this clarity. People don't know what skills or experiences would prepare them for advancement. Development becomes random rather than intentional.

I've seen and used developmental pathway documents for major roles. Each one outlines:

- The key competencies required for the role.
- The typical progression of assignments that prepares someone for the role.
- The training, education, or certifications that support development.
- The approximate timeline for development to recognize individual variation.

These aren't rigid requirements but transparent guidance. They help people develop intentionally toward roles they aspire to fill.

LEADERS TEACHING LEADERS

One of the most powerful development tools is having leaders teach leadership. When senior leaders regularly teach junior leaders, multiple benefits accrue:

- **Teaching deepens learning**: Senior leaders clarify their own thinking by teaching others.
- **Modeling matters**: Junior leaders see senior leaders prioritizing development.
- **Relationships form**: Teaching naturally creates mentoring relationships.
- **Culture reinforces**: The act of teaching leadership communicates that leadership development matters.

Common Pitfalls in Leadership Development

Even well-intentioned development efforts can fail. Watch for the common pitfalls.

DEVELOPMENT AS PERK, NOT PRIORITY

Many organizations treat development as a perk, something offered to high performers or those in leadership's favor. This approach fails because:

- It doesn't develop the people who need development most.
- It creates a perception of favoritism.
- It treats development as optional rather than essential.

Instead, treat development as a priority for everyone. Different people may need different types of development, but everyone should have clear goals and systematic support.

TRAINING WITHOUT APPLICATION

Organizations often send people to training programs but provide no opportunities to apply what they've learned. Therefore, the training is quickly forgotten.

Effective development links learning to application. When someone attends training, immediately provide opportunities to apply new skills: "You just learned about project management, here's a project to manage."

FEEDBACK WITHOUT SUPPORT

Some organizations provide feedback about developmental needs, but no support for addressing them. They tell people what to develop, but not how to develop it.

Effective development pairs feedback with support. "Here's what you need to develop, and here's how we will help you develop it."

PATIENCE WITHOUT ACCOUNTABILITY

Development takes time, but unlimited patience without accountability enables a lack of progress. Some people will avoid development indefinitely if there's no accountability.

Balance patience with accountability. Be patient with the pace of development but hold people accountable for engaging in developmental activities and making progress.

DEVELOPING PEOPLE FOR ROLES THAT DON'T EXIST

Sometimes organizations develop people for leadership roles but have no actual leadership positions for them to fill. The developed people then leave for opportunities elsewhere.

This isn't entirely avoidable, as developed people will always have options elsewhere. But consider:

- Are you creating developmental roles and responsibilities even without formal position changes?
- Are you helping people see career paths forward, even if they require patience?
- Are you genuinely preparing people for advancement, not just keeping them busy?

Your Development Challenge

Leadership development isn't something you do after mastering everything else. It's something to start now, wherever you are in the leadership journey.

If you are an emerging leader with no direct reports, you can still develop future leaders by:

- Mentoring peers who are struggling.
- Sharing what you're learning about leadership.
- Modeling leadership behaviors even without formal authority.

If you're a frontline supervisor, you can systematically develop your team by:

- Holding regular developmental conversations with each team member.
- Creating stretch assignments that develop specific capabilities.
- Providing honest, supportive feedback focused on growth.

If you're a senior leader, you can build organizational development systems by:

- Making development a stated priority with dedicated time and resources.
- Modeling development by teaching and mentoring personally.
- Measuring and rewarding the development of others, not just individual accomplishment.

Whatever your level, ask yourself:

- If I left tomorrow, which leaders would remain?
- What would they be capable of?
- What is my legacy?

Practical Steps: Becoming a Developer of Leaders

If you want to develop future leaders, begin with the following concrete practices.

- **Daily practices**:
  - **Ask developmental questions**: Instead of telling people what to do, ask questions that help them think through problems themselves.

- **Catch people doing things right**: Provide positive feedback on developmental progress, not just task completion.
- **Share your thinking**: When making decisions, explain your reasoning so others learn the decision-making process.

- **Weekly practices**:
  - **Review assignments developmentally**: Before assigning tasks, consider who would benefit most from the developmental opportunity.
  - **Coach, don't just manage**: Spend time coaching at least one person through a challenge that they are facing.
  - **Reflect on your development**: What are you learning? How are you developing? You can't develop others if you're not developing yourself.

- **Monthly practices**:
  - **Conduct developmental one-on-ones**: Meet with each direct report to discuss their development, not just their tasks.
  - **Identify stretch assignments**: Look ahead to identify opportunities that will stretch people beyond their current capabilities.
  - **Evaluate development efforts**: Are you actively developing future leaders, or just managing current operations?

- **Quarterly practices**:
    - **Review developmental progress**: Assess the progress of team members' developmental goals.
    - **Adjust developmental plans**: Based on progress and changing circumstances, adjust developmental focus.
    - **Celebrate developmental milestones**: Publicly recognize achievements.

- **Annual practices**:
    - **Assess organizational development capacity**: How effectively is the organization developing future leaders?
    - **Plan developmental investments**: What training, resources, or programs would enhance development?
    - **Evaluate your legacy**: If you left tomorrow, what leaders would remain? What would they be capable of?

Chapter 8

Bringing It All Together: Your Leadership Philosophy

The seven principles I've explored in this book form a comprehensive framework for leadership excellence. But principles alone don't make a leader.

What makes a leader is how you internalize these concepts, blend them with your own experiences and values, and forge them into a personal leadership philosophy that guides your decisions and actions.

This final chapter is about synthesis, taking what you've learned and making it your own. It's about creating a leadership approach that's authentic to who you are while remaining grounded in proven principles. And it's about ensuring that your leadership philosophy isn't just words on paper but a living framework that evolves with you throughout your career.

The Danger of Borrowed Leadership

Early in my career, I watched a specific leader. He was charismatic, decisive, and commanded respect effortlessly. I tried to emulate his style—the way he spoke in meetings, his direct communication approach, even his body language—and it was a disaster.

What worked naturally for him felt forced and inauthentic coming from me. My team sensed the disconnect. I wasn't being myself; I was performing a role. The leadership principles he employed were sound, but his specific application of those principles was uniquely his. I needed to find my own way to apply those same principles.

The lesson was clear. You can learn from other leaders, but you cannot become them. You must develop your own authentic leadership philosophy.

This is one of the most common mistakes emerging leaders make. They try to copy another leader's style rather than developing their own. They adopt someone else's decision-making process, communication patterns, or team-building approaches without considering whether those methods align with their own personality, values, and context.

Authentic leadership requires self-awareness. You must understand strengths, acknowledge weaknesses, recognize values, and know what drives you. Only then can you take universal leadership principles and apply them in ways that are genuine and effective.

The Components of a Personal Leadership Philosophy

A robust personal leadership philosophy consists of several key components:

- **Core values**: These are the nonnegotiable principles that guide all decisions. They're the lines you won't cross, the standards you won't compromise. In my case, integrity, service, excellence, and empowerment form the foundation of everything I do as a leader.
- **Mission understanding**: How do you define the purpose of leadership? Is it to accomplish specific organizational goals? To develop people? To serve a larger cause? Your philosophy must clearly articulate what you're ultimately trying to achieve. My philosophy focuses on providing opportunities for success.
- **People perspective**: What is your fundamental belief about people? Do you see them as resources to be managed or as individuals to be developed? Underlying assumptions about people will profoundly shape how you lead them. I believe people can be successful regardless of past or present circumstances.
- **Decision-making framework**: How do you approach difficult decisions? What process do you follow? What factors do you weigh? What principles guide you when faced with competing priorities or ethical dilemmas?
- **Growth mindset**: How do you approach your development and that of others? Do you believe leadership capability is fixed or can it be developed? How do you respond to failure, yours and that of others?
- **Leadership style preferences**: While you should be adaptable, you likely have natural preferences. Are you more directive or collaborative? Do you prefer structure or flexibility? Do you lead best through inspiration or through clear expectations? Regardless of style, serve and develop others.

SYNTHESIZING THE SEVEN PRINCIPLES

Here is how the seven principles from this book integrate into a cohesive philosophy:

1. **Mission First, People Always**: Establishes the fundamental tension to be navigated throughout your leadership career. You can't sacrifice mission for people or people for mission; you must accomplish both simultaneously. This principle forces you to think systemically rather than linearly.
2. **Lead by Example**: Defines a personal accountability standard. Before asking anything of a team, ask it of yourself. This principle keeps you honest and builds the credibility necessary for all other principles to work.
3. **Empower and Trust**: Determines how you distribute authority and cultivate ownership. This principle prevents you from becoming a bottleneck and enables the organization to scale beyond your personal capacity.
4. **Discipline and Standards**: Provides the structure within which empowerment occurs. Without this principle, empowerment becomes chaos. With it, empowerment becomes organizational capability.
5. **Communication**: Serves as the connective tissue that makes all other principles possible. You can't lead by example if people don't see it. You can't empower if you don't clearly communicate authority and expectations. You can't maintain standards if you don't communicate them consistently.
6. **Adaptability**: Keeps leadership relevant as circumstances change. This principle prevents philosophy from becoming rigid dogma. It ensures you remain effective across different contexts, challenges, and eras.

7. **Develop Future Leaders**: Extends impact beyond your own tenure. This principle transforms leadership from a personal achievement into a generational legacy. It's how you multiply yourself and ensure continued organizational success.

These seven principles don't exist in isolation—they interact, support, and sometimes create tension with each other. Your leadership philosophy must address how you'll balance and integrate them.

Creating a Personal Leadership Constitution

I recommend creating what I call a *personal leadership constitution*, a written document that articulates your leadership philosophy. This isn't a mission statement or a list of platitudes. It's a practical framework that guides daily decisions and actions.

Here's how to create one.

IDENTIFY CORE VALUES

List three to five absolutely nonnegotiable values. These should be principles you'd uphold even at significant personal cost. For each value, write a brief explanation of what it means to you and why it matters.

When I did this, my values were:

- **Service**: I exist to serve the mission and the people accomplishing it.
- **Excellence**: I will pursue continuous improvement in all things.
- **Empowerment**: I will build capability in others, not dependency.

DEFINE THE LEADERSHIP MISSION

In one or two sentences, articulate the fundamental purpose of your leadership. What are you ultimately trying to accomplish? What impact do you want to have?

My leadership (and life) mission is "To provide people with an opportunity to succeed regardless of their past or present circumstances."

This is my "Why."

ARTICULATE A PEOPLE PHILOSOPHY

Write a paragraph describing your fundamental beliefs about people. What do you believe about human potential, motivation, and development?

For example, my people philosophy is, "People are capable of far more than they or their leaders typically believe. Given clear expectations, proper resources, genuine trust, and appropriate support, most people will rise to challenges and exceed expectations. My job is to create the conditions for that growth, remove obstacles, then get out of the way."

ESTABLISH A DECISION-MAKING FRAMEWORK

Describe the process you'll follow when making difficult decisions, especially when principles seem to conflict. What questions will you ask? What factors will you weigh?

My framework includes these questions:

- Does this decision align with my core values?
- Does it serve both mission and people?

- Am I willing and able to publicly explain and defend this decision?
- What would I advise someone else to do in this situation?
- What's the second-order effect of this decision?

DEFINE LEADERSHIP COMMITMENTS

List specific, actionable commitments that flow from your values and philosophy. These are the tangible behaviors you'll demonstrate consistently.

Examples of my commitments:

- I will never ask my team to do something I'm unwilling to do.
- I will communicate directly and honestly, even when it's uncomfortable.
- I will admit mistakes quickly and publicly.
- I will praise others and celebrate them publicly, I will correct privately.
- I will invest time in developing every person on my team.
- I will maintain the same standards for everyone, including myself.

ACKNOWLEDGE YOUR DEVELOPMENT AREAS

Identify two to three areas where you need to grow as a leader. This honest self-assessment keeps you humble and focused on continuous improvement.

My current development areas:

- To eliminate the "fragmented day" by dedicating specific blocks of time to high-priority leadership tasks, ensuring that "noise" does not crowd out strategic thinking.
- Patience with processes that slow down decision-making.
- Delegating tasks that I enjoy doing myself.

When Philosophy Is Tested

Your leadership philosophy will face its greatest tests during times of crisis, when the pressure is highest, and the stakes are greatest. These are the moments that reveal whether the philosophy is deeply held or merely aspirational.

I've often faced situations that seem difficult. Emergency projects, outages, or dangerous missions. The mission-first part of me wants to start immediately and get the work done. The people-always part of me wants to protect the team from unnecessary danger and potential burnout.

I always go back to my philosophy that mission and people aren't competing priorities. The question isn't whether to approve the work, but how to approve it in a way that maximizes mission success while minimizing unnecessary negative impact to the team.

Just slow down. Take a breath and look at options. You can bring in additional resources, adjust the approach, and ensure that contingencies are planned for. It requires holding the tension between mission and people rather than choosing one over the other.

A personal philosophy should help you navigate these difficult moments—not by providing easy answers, but by clarifying the questions you need to ask and the factors you need to weigh.

Leadership Philosophy Across Contexts

One of the challenges you'll face is applying a leadership philosophy across different organizations, teams, missions, and levels of responsibility.

The principles remain constant, but the application must adapt.

When I transitioned from the small school district to a much larger one, my leadership philosophy didn't change, but my application of it had to evolve significantly.

In the small district, I could maintain personal relationships with every member of the technology team. I knew their families, their career aspirations, their strengths, and their struggles. I could lead by direct personal influence.

In the large district, that level of personal connection with everyone was impossible. I had to develop leaders who would carry my philosophy throughout the organization. I had to create systems and structures that embodied my values rather than relying solely on personal relationships.

The principle of *mission first, people always* remained the same. But the practice shifted from personal care to building a culture of care throughout the organization.

A leadership philosophy must be both firm and flexible; firm in its core principles, flexible in its application.

The Evolution of Your Philosophy

Leadership isn't static. It should evolve as you gain experience, face new challenges, and learn from successes and failures.

My philosophy today is substantially more nuanced than it was when I was a young team leader. The core values remain the same, but my understanding of how to apply them has deepened. I've learned that leadership principles I thought contradicted each other are actually complementary. I've discovered blind spots I didn't know I had. I've had to adjust approaches that worked in one context but failed in another.

This evolution is healthy and necessary. A leadership philosophy that never changes suggests you're not learning from experience.

The key is to ensure your philosophy evolves through genuine learning and reflection, not through compromise of core values or expedient rationalization of questionable decisions.

BUILDING A LEADERSHIP LIBRARY

Throughout your career, continue learning from other leaders, both those observed directly and those encountered through books, podcasts, and other media. But consume this content through the filter of your own developing philosophy. Ask yourself:

- How does this leader's approach align with or differ from my philosophy?
- What can I learn from them without compromising my authenticity?
- How would I apply this principle or technique in my own context?
- What aspects of their leadership should I avoid or modify?

The goal isn't to become them. It's to continuously refine your own approach by learning from their experiences.

Your Leadership Legacy

Ultimately, your leadership philosophy determines your leadership legacy. Years from now, when people who worked for you think about your leadership, what will they remember? How will they describe what it was like to work for you? What lessons will they carry forward into their own leadership?

A legacy isn't built on what you accomplish personally; it's built on what you enable others to accomplish and how you shape them as leaders.

The first time someone tells you that you helped show them how to be a good leader, that you made them want to take on a leadership position, or when someone comes back to ask for advice about a situation, that moment will change you. It crystallized for me what leadership is really about.

It's not about the projects you complete or the budgets you manage or the awards you win. It's about how you shape the people you lead and the leaders they become.

A leadership philosophy is the vehicle through which you create that impact.

From Philosophy to Practice

A leadership philosophy is only valuable if it shapes daily actions. Here's how to translate philosophy into practice:

- **Daily application**: Start each day by reviewing your leadership commitments. End each day by reflecting on how well you lived them. This daily discipline keeps the philosophy front-of-mind.
- **Decision filter**: When facing a significant decision, explicitly run it through your framework. Ask yourself, "Is this decision consistent with my leadership philosophy?" If not, either change the decision or be prepared to explain why this situation warrants an exception.

- **Team transparency**: Share your leadership philosophy with the team. Let them know what you value, how you make decisions, and what they can expect from you. This transparency builds trust and allows the team to hold you accountable.
- **Regular review**: Quarterly, review your leadership philosophy. Are you living it consistently? Has your understanding evolved? Do any components need adjustment based on new experiences or insights?
- **Seek feedback**: Ask trusted colleagues and team members for honest feedback on whether your actions align with your stated philosophy. The gap between who we think we are and how others experience us is often illuminating.

The Journey Forward

You now have a comprehensive framework for leadership, seven core principles that—when integrated into a personal philosophy and applied with consistency and authenticity—will help make you an effective leader in any context.

But understanding these principles intellectually is just the beginning. The real work starts now, in the process of developing a personal leadership constitution:

- Begin applying these principles in your daily leadership.
- Seek feedback and adjust your approach.
- Invest in developing the leaders around you.
- Commit to continuous learning and growth.

Leadership is not a destination. It's a journey of continuous development. There will always be new challenges to face, new skills to develop, and new insights to gain.

The question isn't whether you're a perfect leader. None of us are. The question is whether you're committed to serving those you lead, growing as a leader, and leaving your organization and people better than you found them.

If you commit to that journey, equipped with the principles in this book and guided by your own authentic leadership philosophy, you'll make a profound difference in the lives of those you lead and the missions you serve.

That's what leadership is ultimately about. It's not about your success, but the success you enable in others.

Afterword

The Future

Early in my career, I measured success by what I accomplished. How many missions did I support? How many systems did I implement? How many problems did I solve?

Now I measure success differently. I measure it by the leaders I've developed. By the team members who advanced to greater responsibility. By the people who are now developing their own future leaders.

This shift from personal accomplishment to others' development is the essence of servant leadership. It's also the ultimate expression of mission focus, because the long-term goal of every organization should be to develop leaders who can carry the mission forward after current leaders are gone.

Begin Today

Leadership development can seem overwhelming. Where do you start? What if you make mistakes? What if you invest in someone who doesn't develop as expected? These fears paralyze many leaders into inaction. They wait until they have perfect systems, complete knowledge, or ideal conditions before beginning to develop others.

Don't wait.

Begin today with what you have, where you are. Have one developmental conversation this week. Give one piece of coaching feedback. Create one stretch assignment. Share one lesson you've learned. Leadership development doesn't require perfection; it requires commitment. It doesn't demand complete systems; it demands consistent action. It doesn't need ideal conditions; it needs leaders who care enough to invest in others' growth.

The leader you develop this year might become the leader who develops dozens of others over the next decade. The investment you make today might ripple forward for generations. Your greatest achievement as a leader won't be what you accomplish personally. It will be what the leaders you develop accomplish long after you're gone.

That's your legacy.

Start building it today.

This book is intended as an introduction to integrating military leadership principles with servant leadership ideals. Each chapter has explored one key principle at a foundational level. There are other books that go deeper into these principles. But you don't need to wait to read those books to begin applying what you've learned here. Start today. Choose one principle and focus on it this week. Next week, add another. Gradually build these principles into your daily leadership practice.

The best time to become a better leader was yesterday. The second-best time is now.

As you move forward in your leadership journey, remember that the principles in this book are not rules to follow rigidly but guidelines to adapt wisely. Your leadership is uniquely yours and is shaped by your experiences, refined by your values, and expressed through your authentic voice.

Serve faithfully. Lead authentically. Develop others generously. That's the essence of great leadership.

About the Author

Robert Moore has spent more than three decades learning leadership the hard way—in uniform, in combat, in boardrooms, and in the halls of public education. He began his career as an enlisted soldier in the United States Army, where he discovered early that leadership is less about rank and more about responsibility. That conviction carried him through a commissioned officer career, multiple overseas and combat deployments, and eventually into senior executive roles leading complex organizations far beyond the military.

After leaving active duty, Robert brought the same discipline and people-first philosophy to the civilian sector, serving in chief information officer roles across public education. He has led in large, mission-driven organizations through periods of significant change—building teams, developing emerging leaders, and navigating the kind of institutional challenges that test whether a leader's values are real or merely decorative.

What has mattered most, across every role and every organization, is not what he accomplished but who he helped grow. A mentor once told him that the measure of a leader is not what they achieve while they are present, but what continues after they are gone. That idea became the foundation for this book.

The Leaders You Leave Behind is Robert's attempt to put into plain language what he has observed, practiced, and learned across a career that has taken him from basic training to the executive suite.

It is written for leaders at every level . It is for those just starting out, those in the middle of the grind, and those preparing to hand something meaningful off to the next generation.

Robert continues to mentor leaders across sectors. He lives and works with the belief that every organization's greatest investment is the people it develops and that the best leaders measure their legacy not in titles held, but in leaders left behind.

www.ingramcontent.com/pod-product-compliance
Lightning Source LLC
LaVergne TN
LVHW010654110826
845149LV00014B/3076

* 9 7 9 8 9 9 4 7 5 0 3 1 5 *